*Aging
and
Retirement*

BROOKS/COLE SERIES IN SOCIAL GERONTOLOGY

Vern Bengtson, *University of Southern California*
Series Editor

HEALTH AND AGING
Tom Hickey, *University of Michigan*

ENVIRONMENT AND AGING
M. Powell Lawton, *Philadelphia Geriatric Center*

LAST CHAPTERS: A SOCIOLOGY OF AGING AND DYING
Victor W. Marshall, *University of Toronto and McMaster University*

AGING AND RETIREMENT
Anne Foner, *Rutgers University*
Karen Schwab, *Social Security Administration, Washington, D.C.*

ROLE TRANSITIONS IN LATER LIFE
Linda K. George, *Duke University Medical Center*

STRATIFICATION AMONG THE AGED
James J. Dowd, *University of Georgia*

Aging and Retirement

Anne Foner

Rutgers University

Karen Schwab

Social Security Administration
Washington, D.C.

Brooks/Cole Publishing Company
Monterey, California

Brooks/Cole Publishing Company
A Division of Wadsworth, Inc.

Printed in the United States of America

10 9 8 7 6 5 4 3 2 1

Library of Congress Cataloging in Publication Data

Foner, Anne.
    Aging and retirement.

    (Brooks/Cole series in social gerontology)
    Bibliography: p.
    Includes index.
    1. Retirement—United States 2. Aged—United
States. 3. Gerontology—United States. I. Schwab,
Karen, 1946–   joint author. II. Title.
III. Series.
HQ1062.F59   305.2'6'0973   80-24765
ISBN 0-8185-0444-7

Acquisition Editor: *Todd Lueders*
Manuscript Editor: *Julie Segedy*
Production Editor: *Fiorella Ljunggren*
Series Design: *John Edeen*
Typesetting: *Graphic Typesetting Service, Los Angeles, California*

Foreword

Retirement is increasingly an *expectable* life event. Today, unlike only a half-century ago, most of those in the work force can anticipate living years, even decades, after completing their occupational careers. These are the "golden years"—or so advertisements for savings and loan associations and retirement communities tell us.

Yet retirement, even if increasingly expectable, remains a paradox in contemporary industrialized social settings. It is feared by many and misunderstood by most of those individuals in the work force today. It is the source of concern for policymakers and politicians involved in charting social and economic problems of the next decades.

The signal contribution of this book is its success in stating clearly the multiple facets of complex retirement dilemmas. The authors bring to their subject a wealth of data and conceptual tools that illuminate current policy debates about retirement and income support. Anne Foner and Karen Schwab are sociologists who have gone beyond narrow disciplinary boundaries to provide a comprehensive view of retirement.

The perspective taken by Foner and Schwab addresses explicitly the dual nature of the retirement dilemma. On the individual level, the authors note, retirement means a major change for the person: a discontinuity in roles, with few clear normative expectations; a reduction in obvious social rewards in the new role; and few opportunities for learning the new role in advance. On the societal level, retirement allows an orderly turnover in the inevitable succession of generations but presents an economic challenge in terms of support for ever-larger groups of "nonproductive" members of the society. Both individual and societal levels of analysis, Foner and Schwab emphasize, are necessary if we are to adequately understand current policy debates concerning the challenges of retirement.

This book should be required reading for all policymakers involved in retirement issues; legislative analysts will probably find Chapter 7 particularly useful. The book should also be read by those facing retirement in the near future; they will probably spend most time on Chapters 5 and 8. Employers interested in research findings on older workers will learn much from Chapter 2. And most readers will enjoy the careful examination of myths and stereotypes about aging, work, and retirement presented throughout the book.

This volume is one of the Series in Social Gerontology offered by Brooks/Cole Publishing Company. The books in this series review the state of the art in nine topical areas, for audiences of students, practitioners, policymakers, and researchers—as well as for individuals who are themselves making the transition into the later years. Volumes in the series address topics of health and aging, role transitions and stress, death and dying, environmental issues in aging, and social power and status.

The need for such a series of volumes is apparent from recent changes involving applications of the scientific method to the study of aging and social problems. Perhaps the most significant of these changes is the increase in the range of problems mandated for social-policy intervention. From many sectors of contemporary society, we see evidence of urgent demands for policy-relevant information on aging. But at the same time there has been development of more and more sophisticated theory and research in aging. One effect of these changes has been a blurring of professional boundary lines and a growing recognition of the interdependence of "basic" and "applied" research. As Foner and Schwab note, social scientists and policymakers are increasingly aware that much of their work is interrelated and that their interests are often mutual. It is therefore necessary for both to learn the vocabulary and perspectives of the other.

Four themes emerging in the last decade are reflected in the Brooks/Cole Series in Social Gerontology. Each is aptly illustrated by Foner and Schwab in their presentation of aging, work, and retirement. The first concerns *the interplay between basic and applied knowledge* in social gerontology. Since nothing may be quite so practical as a good theory, the current demand for policy-relevant research in aging gives special urgency to the need for concise models that summarize as well as predict.

A second theme is *the necessity of both micro- and macro-level analysis* in gerontology. Foner and Schwab's treatment exemplifies the advantages of combining both microsocial and macrosocial perspectives on retirement while also illustrating the complexity that has made such dual-level analysis rare, even in social gerontology.

Third is *the importance of continuity as well as change* as a framework from which to view aging. Detriment and loss are the stereotypic consequences of changes associated with aging; but, as Foner and Schwab point out, these must be considered along with the continuities of past coping behavior and competence—as well as the new opportunities of freedom and change brought on by seniorhood and retirement. Foner and Schwab note several ways in which retirees employ resources that are frequently overlooked, sometimes even by themselves.

A fourth perspective involves *explicit comparative analysis* of aging in various social settings. Old age and retirement vary by historical and cultural context, and, as Foner and Schwab observe, the population of today's aged is incredibly diverse and quite different from the modal situation of previous historical periods. Therefore, we need to make explicit comparisons among social groups—defined by social class, ethnicity, and race—rather than mistakenly assume that all older people are alike.

This is an intriguing book—a model of what the sociological imagination can and should do with a life-course problem. Readers will find this presentation personally relevant as well as intellectually enlightening. For, when we come to understand the retirement patterns of today, we may be able to foresee our own retirement transitions tomorrow.

Vern L. Bengtson
Series Editor

Preface

The fact that the vast majority of people around age 65 now retire from their customary work roles is a modern phenomenon. This development in our society within the last three decades has, not surprisingly, aroused the interest of scholars, professionals dealing with older people, and the public at large. Along with this increasing interest in retirement, a set of beliefs has emerged about the reasons for people's retiring and the consequences of retirement. As it turns out, many of these beliefs—"what everyone knows"— are ill founded. But even as social-science research has uncovered myths about the impact of retirement on the individual, the impact of mass retirement on the society is a growing concern.

In this book we deal with both issues. We review and interpret research that focuses on the retirement process and on people's lives in retirement— that is, the reasons people retire when they do, their activities as retirees, their reactions to retired life, and the individual and social factors associated with either a good or an unsatisfactory life in retirement. We also look at the broad social, economic, and demographic factors that led to the institutionalization of retirement, that currently create problems for retirement policy, and that promise to shape the retirement role and policy in the future.

A motif running through the book is the dynamic interplay between the individual and the society. We show how public attitudes to the retirement role, as well as the way in which the individual fills the role and reacts to retired life, are influenced by social factors and changes in the social environment. In turn, individual behavior and attitudes affect the society. Individual decisions about retiring before the "normal" retirement age can add up to a ground swell that upsets institutional plans and requires adjustment in public policy just as individual responses to retirement serve to define and redefine the retirement role.

We have grounded much of our analysis in empirical research, using the most up-to-date data that were available at the time of writing. We have included a good deal of material about the social security system because it is such a potent influence on all aspects of retirement.* In pulling together and trying to understand the different strands of research, we have been guided by the age-stratification perspective. From a structural point of view, this means viewing the stratum of retired people against the background of all other age strata in the society. In dynamic terms, it means understanding that responses to retirement are influenced by the individual's previous life history. It also means keeping in mind that the collective history of today's cohorts of retirees—the cohorts on which so much of what we know about retirement is based—is different from that of earlier cohorts of retirees and also different from the biographies of oncoming cohorts of retirees. In short, when they retire, the undergraduates of today are sure to confront changes in the retirement role and changes in the society.

Aging and Retirement is designed to serve the needs of undergraduate students in aging, social gerontology, and public policy. We also hope that the book will be useful to the growing number of professionals in the field.

We have been fortunate in our colleagues who have taken time from their busy schedules to read an earlier draft of this book. We are especially grateful to Professor Matilda White Riley, presently Associate Director, Social and Behavioral Research, National Institute on Aging, for her encouragement and insightful comments; Joan Waring for her critical reading of our earlier efforts; Lola Irelan, Director of the Retirement History Study, Social Security Administration; and Lenore E. Bixby, now retired, former Chief, Division of Retirement and Survivors Studies, Social Security Administration, for their important suggestions. We are grateful to members of our families for their continued support; a special thanks goes to Karen's husband, Dennis Reeder, for his help in computerizing the indexes. We are also indebted to Arthur Norris of the National Institute on Aging for providing us with important data and to Robert C. Atchley of Miami University and Stephen R. McConnell of the University of Southern California for their thoughtful reading. Vern Bengtson, Series Editor, offered understanding and reassurance, and Todd Lueders of Brooks/Cole helped smooth the production of our book. To them, too, our sincere thanks.

Anne Foner
Karen Schwab

---

*This book was co-authored by Karen Schwab in her private capacity. No official support or endorsement by the Social Security Administration is intended or should be inferred.

Contents

Introduction

Who has a stake in **retirement**?[1] Not just the millions of former workers over 60 now out of the labor force. Nor even just those on the threshold of retirement.[2] Retirement affects almost everyone in the society: people in their forties and fifties who want to move into positions now held by older workers; young people awaiting job openings; and anyone whose current payroll taxes contribute to the solvency of the **social security** system. Also concerned are the policymakers who determine rules about age of eligibility for retirement benefits or criteria for older workers remaining on the job, who set rates of payroll deductions and of benefit levels, and who decide about mandatory retirement.

There is much interest in retirement partly because it seems beset by problems—problems for individuals trying to negotiate a smooth transition from a life of work to one of no work and reduced income and problems for the society paying pension benefits to the growing numbers of retirees. Even

---

[1] The terms that appear in boldface are defined in the Glossary at the end of the book.

[2] In this chapter, *retirement* refers to withdrawal from the labor force. In Chapter 3, other definitions of retirement are discussed.

if there were no problems, the study of retirement would still be important. Sociologists, for example, are interested in the everyday life of people and try to explore what is under the surface of people's lives. They examine how people's ways of thinking and acting are affected by their employment status, their occupation or former occupation, their age, sex, or ethnicity, for example. Retirement is currently the accepted practice for older workers, and sociologists have turned the spotlight on patterns of work and retirement to explore the accuracy of widely held beliefs about retirement and to heighten our understanding of the causes and consequences of retirement in modern society.

In this chapter we will discuss how retirement fits into the broad social setting of modern, complex, industrial society. We will show that retirement as the customary pattern for older people is relatively new; we will describe some of the economic and social factors that account for the institutionalization of retirement; and we will indicate some of the problems thought to be associated with retirement.

Retirement—A Normal Life Stage?

Shakespeare said "All the world's a stage, and all the men and women merely players. They have their exits and their entrances" (*As You Like It,* II, vii). We tend to think of retirement as one of the exits people must make, one of several "normal" stages in the life course. Just as we expect children and adolescents to go to school and then to graduate from school, we expect adult men (and, increasingly, adult women) to engage in paid work and then to withdraw from the **labor force** at around the age of 65. These expectations are based on actual practices: most men and women in their sixties *are* no longer in the work force. Considering all those who are 65 and over—some 9.8 million men and 14.3 million women in 1978—about 20% of the men and less than 10% of the women are still in the labor force—that is, are presently working or seeking work. The pattern of withdrawal from the labor force in the later years has also occurred in most other industrial countries (Riley & Foner, 1968; U.S. Bureau of the Census, 1979b; International Labour Office, 1978).

It wasn't always this way. In the past, far fewer people lived to old age than today. But those who did survive to old age tended to remain in the labor force past the age of 65. For example, in the United States in 1900, of the 1.6 million men 65 and over, two-thirds were still in the labor force; in 1920, 60% of the older men were still economically active. Relatively few women worked at paid employment during those years; the proportion of women age 65 and over in the labor force at the turn of the century was about 10%. Significantly, this proportion has remained virtually unchanged throughout the century, even

TABLE 1-1. *Labor Force Participation Rates, United States 1900–1976 (Percent in Labor Force)*

Sex and Age	1900	1920	1940	1944	1950	1955	1960		1970	1976
Both sexes	55.0	55.8	55.9	63.1	58.3	58.7	57.4		60.3	61.2
Males										
14+	87.7	85.9	83.9	89.8	84.4	83.6	79.7	16+	79.2	76.9
14–17	63.6	52.6	44.2	70.0	53.2	49.5	34.4	16–17	46.7	48.4
18–19							73.1		68.8	72.1
20–24	91.7	91.0	96.1	98.5	89.0	90.8	88.9		85.1	85.2
25–34	96.3	97.2	98.1	99.0	96.2	97.7	96.4		95.0	94.2
35–44			98.5	99.0	97.6	98.4	96.4		95.7	94.6
45–54	93.3	93.8	95.5	97.1	95.8	96.4	94.3		92.9	90.6
55–64			87.2	92.1	87.0	88.3	85.2		81.5	73.5
65+	68.3	60.1	45.0	52.2	45.8	40.6	32.2		25.8	19.4
Females										
14+	20.4	24.1	28.2	36.8	33.1	34.8	36.1	16+	42.8	46.8
14–17	26.8	28.4	23.3	42.0	31.5	29.9	20.8	16–17	34.6	40.6
18–19							51.0		53.4	58.9
20–24	32.1	38.1	49.5	55.0	46.1	46.0	46.1		57.5	65.0
25–34	18.1	22.4	35.2	39.0	34.0	34.9	35.8		44.8	56.9
35–44			28.8	40.5	39.1	41.6	43.1		50.9	57.6
45–54	14.1	17.1	24.3	35.8	38.0	43.8	49.3		54.0	54.6
55–64			18.7	25.4	27.0	32.5	36.7		42.5	40.7
65+	9.1	8.0	7.4	9.8	9.7	10.6	10.5		9.2	7.8

Adapted from *Aging and Society. Vol. 1: An Inventory of Research Findings,* by M. W. Riley and A. Foner. Copyright 1968 by the Russell Sage Foundation. Used by permission. Additional data are from U.S. Bureau of the Census, 1977, p. 387.

though women's overall labor force participation rates have increased so markedly (see Table 1-1).

Retirement is also not the typical pattern in countries less industrialized than the United States. In the 1950s and early 1960s, when the majority of older men in the United States were out of the labor force, most males 65 and over were reported to be in the labor force in semi-industrial and in predominantly agricultural countries (Riley & Foner, 1968). As recently as 1975, labor force participation rates of older men in the less developed regions of the world were relatively high. In South Asia and Africa, for example, about 60% of the older men were reported to be in the labor force in 1975 (see Tables 1-2 and 1-3).

Of course, many older people do withdraw from productive work in less industrialized countries, but their withdrawal is often gradual. This is facilitated by the nature of agricultural employment, the type of work in which most of these people are engaged. Typically, agricultural work includes many different jobs that must be done, so it is possible for a person to gradually

TABLE 1-2. *Labor Force Participation Rates of Older Workers, 1975 (Percent in the Labor Force)*

Major Region	45–54	55–64	65+
	Males		
World	94.44	80.98	38.69
More developed regions	93.82	75.26	22.95
Less developed regions	94.79	84.42	52.88
USSR	92.43	56.30	10.60
Europe	94.14	76.78	21.70
North America	92.91	80.44	23.94
Oceania	95.13	83.66	25.36
Latin America	92.90	79.41	45.71
East Asia	94.57	82.27	46.81
South Asia	95.30	86.56	58.82
Africa	96.42	89.78	61.77
	Females		
World	51.60	33.34	11.76
More developed regions	60.39	31.85	7.55
Less developed regions	45.65	34.49	17.07
USSR	84.05	18.02	3.67
Europe	49.44	31.55	7.63
North America	57.30	42.86	8.60
Oceania	42.90	25.20	5.18
Latin America	21.31	15.10	7.06
East Asia	58.64	41.63	19.43
South Asia	40.94	31.77	15.05
Africa	45.36	37.71	19.78

Adapted from International Labour Office, 1978, p. 8.

switch from strenuous to easier tasks. Thus, work can usually be found for older people either in actual production or among marginal jobs (Goody, 1976; International Labour Office, 1978).

Retiring from the labor force as the customary practice in the person's later years is thus associated with industrialism. Many aspects of industrial societies seem related to the decline in older men's labor force participation. A key factor has been the dramatic decline in agricultural employment. In the United States, the proportion of all workers engaged in agriculture has dropped from more than 50% in 1870 to 38% in 1900 to only about 4% in 1975. Paralleling the decline in agriculture has been a less marked but still important decline in nonagricultural self-employment. Further, while agriculture and self-employment have been contracting, the concentration of many workers in large firms has been increasing. In these large firms, hiring and firing are guided by organizational rules, and the pace and scheduling of work are not set by the workers themselves. The growth of large-scale enterprises has meant that fewer people are free to make their own choice to continue work, retire, or taper off gradually.

TABLE 1-3. International Trends in Labor Force Participation Rates of Older Workers, 1950–2000

Major Region	1950	1975	2000 (Projected)
World		*Males*	
45–54	96	94	93
55–64	89	81	75
65 +	58	39	27
Developed countries			
45–54	95	94	93
55–64	86	75	69
65 +	44	23	17
Developing countries			
45–54	97	95	93
55–64	91	84	77
65 +	69	53	34
World		*Females*	
45–54	42	52	51
55–64	31	33	31
65 +	16	12	8
Developed countries			
45–54	44	60	67
55–64	32	32	35
65 +	17	8	6
Developing countries			
45–54	39	46	44
55–64	31	35	30
65 +	16	17	10

Adapted from International Labour Office, 1978, pp. 8–9.

In general, the job market has not been favorable to older workers. For one thing, there has been a steady rise in the educational level of the whole work force; this has occurred primarily because of the entry of younger, better educated workers. Older workers have had, on the average, fewer years of schooling than younger workers, and the training of older workers is less recent than younger workers'. In the 19th century, education was not an important criterion for many jobs, and the gap between younger and older workers was less marked because the educational upgrading of the work force was less rapid than now. In other words, each new **cohort** of workers entering the labor force did not have much more schooling than the older cohorts. But consider the educational levels of a younger and older cohort[3] in 1978. Among those 25–29, 46% had one or more years of college while only about 5% had an eighth-grade education or less; among those 55 and over, 18% had one or

[3]A cohort is an aggregate of individuals who were born in the same time interval.

more years of college while 36% had only an eighth-grade education or less (U.S. Bureau of the Census, 1979b). These statistics are important because many employers use education as a criterion for hiring because of the actual job requirements or because education serves as a useful screening device. Employers also frequently want to ease out older workers in favor of younger workers with higher levels of education and more up-to-date training.

In addition to the lack of educational credentials, widespread beliefs (some of them ill founded) about the disadvantages of hiring or keeping older workers on the job operate to handicap them in the job market. Employers often believe that older workers are either incapable of meeting the physical requirements of the job, cannot conform to company standards, are unable to learn new techniques, are expensive, or simply stand in the way of promoting younger, presumably more innovative employees.

Specific employer practices and public programs have also played an important part in facilitating the withdrawal of older workers from the labor force. Until very recently, a substantial number of workers were required to leave their jobs when they reached 65, sometimes even earlier. (As a result of recent federal legislation, employing organizations with **mandatory retirement** may not set the age of retirement below 70, in most instances.) Yet, whether mandatory retirement provisions apply or not, there are often other, indirect pressures on the worker to leave the job. In fact, many workers leave their jobs before age 65. Some jobs are tough and unpleasant—for instance, many jobs in steel mills or auto plants—so workers are willing to retire if they can be assured an adequate retirement income. Other workers have health problems that make working difficult. Still others feel pressure from younger workers to step aside and make opportunity for them. Whatever the reason, the availability of public and private pensions permits many of the older workers to withdraw from the labor force. In the past, most workers who wanted to leave their jobs had to depend on their families to support them. The extension of social security and of various private and public pension plans today affords an alternative source of income to more than 90% of older workers. In May 1979, for example, more than 18 million retired workers were receiving social security benefits (*Social Security Bulletin,* 1979). Over 2½ million disabled workers and more than 13 million dependents and survivors were also receiving benefits under Old Age, Survivor, Disability and Health Insurance (**OASDHI**) coverage. In addition, a substantial minority of the retired workers were receiving private pension benefits.

As you can see, a variety of related factors—the decline of agriculture and of self-employment, the growth of large-scale, technologically advanced enterprises, the educational upgrading of occupations, the competitive status of older workers, specific personnel policies, and publicly supported programs—have all played a part in the long-term decline in the labor force participation of older men (see Riley, Johnson, & Foner, 1972, Chapter 5). But what has only been implied so far is undoubtedly a key feature of industrial society: productivity per worker in the United States has been so high in the past that much of the existing demand for goods and services could be met without the economic activity of older (and younger) workers.[4]

In a sense retirement can be considered a social invention that has evolved to deal with some of the developments of industrial societies. But there are alternatives for patterning the work life of individuals: more drastic shortening of hours, extending vacations, and interspersing periods of education, leisure, and work throughout the life course rather than concentrating education at the beginning and nonproductive roles at the end. Whether such alternatives are feasible, whether older people are likely to continue to leave the labor force in large numbers, or whether society will still be able to do without the services of older workers are still open questions. Much depends on changes in the age composition of the population, changes in the qualifications of the whole work force, and the general state of the economy. We will deal with these questions later on.

Retirement—A Troubled Life Stage?

Retirement is the standard pattern for older people in the United States, and many scholars and practitioners in the helping professions are concerned about the impact of retirement on individuals. Making the transition from work to retirement involves sharp and abrupt changes in a person's life—what sociologists call **role discontinuities** (Riley & Waring, 1976). There is considerable evidence that many kinds of changes—and apparently even some desirable changes—can affect people's mental and physical functioning. The birth of a child, the death of a family member, promotion to or loss of a job all require readjustments in life circumstances, and many such events have been found to be related to a variety of physical disorders and psychological impairments (Liem & Liem, 1978).

Clearly, retirement constitutes a life event that might be expected to create problems. The particular problems associated with retirement can be appreciated by comparing the transition to retirement with another major life transition marked by role discontinuities. The transition from adolescence to adulthood, for example, is also characterized by sharp changes in the **roles** a person fills and in what is expected of him or her. As adolescents, we are often dependent; as adults, we are expected to be independent. As adolescents, we have had few responsibilities; as adults, we assume many responsibilities. And, in the transition to adulthood, people must often learn several new roles simultaneously: worker, marital partner, and parent.

[4]The fact that productivity has been so high does not mean that the overall size of the labor force has declined. Indeed, the size of the total labor force in relation to the population has been fairly stable throughout the century and may possibly have increased somewhat. A major counterbalance to the decreasing participation of older men has been the increase in labor force participation of women.

Difficult as the adjustments may be for the young adult, they seem less troublesome than those facing the retiree. Young adults assume roles that are highly valued by the society; but retirees relinquish these highly valued roles and take on roles that may repudiate some deeply held values. For example, many of today's retirees have been brought up to believe in the *work ethic*— that is, to believe that work is good, moral, and right—and to feel that the measure of a man is in the work he does. For these men, retirement, with its emphasis on leisure, would seem difficult to enjoy. Further, whereas adolescents relinquish the roles of dependent child or student to take on new roles with quite clear expectations, retired people relinquish highly structured work roles with *no* clear expectations about what they are to do as retirees. After the first few weeks of freedom from strict schedules—perhaps getting up late rather than going to work—retirees are faced with the problem of fashioning a new way of life. They are told "Be active," but there are no clear guidelines for specific activities or for the restructuring of the remainder of their lives (Rosow, 1974). As Erich Fromm (1965) pointed out years ago, people often wish to escape the burdens of too much freedom. Perhaps many retirees also feel there is too much freedom, too many choices to make.

To continue the analogy, adolescents making the transition to adult roles of worker, spouse, and parent, are assuming roles with generally higher **social rewards** than those of the roles they have relinquished. In contrast, retirees experience a reduction in social rewards: in their incomes, in their prestige, and in their power. Thus, even though some retirees make plans for enriching their lives, they do not always have the means to realize these plans.

Finally, the transition to retirement these days is generally fairly abrupt and probably more sudden than the transition to adulthood. While most young adults have had the opportunity to practice their adult roles in advance—many teenagers, for example, have had paying jobs, and, through dating or living together, many of them have had **anticipatory socialization** for marital roles (Foner, 1978)—opportunities for advance preparation for retirement or for gradual retirement are limited. Only a minority of retirees have had preretirement counseling. There have been few **role models** from whom to learn the retirement role (at least among the early generations of retirees). Few companies permit workers to taper off work gradually. Indeed, for many retirees, it has been work on Friday, but no work and no place to go on the following Monday.

To sum up, the transition to retirement lacks many of the conditions that social scientists have found to be important for learning and fitting into new roles. Instead, there are sharp discontinuities in roles, without clear norms about what is expected of retirees, a reduction in social rewards, and, especially for the early cohorts of retirees, few opportunities for learning the role in advance or gradually easing into it. It is no surprise that it was commonly believed that people would languish in retirement and that illness and premature death would result.

According to current evidence, there *is* a relationship between retirement and poor health, but not as usually stated. If anything, it appears to be poor health, or the *perception* that one's health is poor, that is likely to lead to retirement rather than retirement causing poor health. Further, the pessimistic predictions about how people would react to retirement seem to have been unwarranted, at least in the 1970s. Thus, despite transition difficulties, most retirees seem to be satisfied with life in retirement. There are many reasons for these positive responses, which we will discuss in detail in later chapters.

In trying to understand why retirees react to the retirement role as they do, characteristics of individuals—their health, income, or attitudes—tend to be accentuated. Important as these are, we propose that the overall societal context in which retirement takes place must also be considered. For one thing, a person's income depends a great deal on federal and business pension policies. Also, as the number of retired people has increased, societal facilities have mushroomed. During the 1960s and 1970s, manufacturers have become increasingly aware of the mass market that older people represent and have targeted products for this market; recreational centers for retired people have sprouted; and retirement communities have emerged as residential havens for the retiree. Indeed, the sheer number of retirees provides an environment in which people can learn from each other and can collectively create norms for the retirement role (see Sumner, 1959). While the impact of these conditions has been little studied, we believe that in the last few decades the societal environment has become increasingly favorable to retirees. As we will discuss in Chapter 6, this climate has been one factor in the positive responses of retirees to their new roles.

Retirement and the Society

Just as the societal changes in the last few decades have been quite favorable for retirees, there is reason to believe that new problems await the society and future retirees. In anticipation of these new difficulties, public policies are already being altered.

The broad issue for the future is how to best support a growing number of economically unproductive older people. Because social security benefits provide the main economic support for retired people, a major focus has been on the solvency of the social security system. Essentially this system is a **pay-as-you-go tax and benefit scheme**. It is not like an insurance system where each worker contributes to his or her own retirement fund. Thus, the current population of workers contributes to the benefits of the current population of retirees through payroll tax deductions—in other words, a transfer of funds from generation to generation. In past decades the growing number of working-age people provided an expanding base for tax collection with which to support retirees. In addition, economic growth, which helped to raise hourly wages, has made it possible to raise social security benefit levels and to increase the number of persons receiving benefits. As economist Paul Samuelson noted, the system has been one in which everybody got back more than they put into the retirement insurance system (Kreps, 1976).

Even if economic growth continues this way, further increases in social security benefits are not at all assured. For in about five or six decades hence, the number of working-age people relative to the number of retirees is expected to decline. On the one hand, the number of older people in the population will be increasing; on the other hand, fertility rates have been declining, thus reducing the proportion of younger people in the entire population. When the baby-boom cohort—the bumper crop of babies born in the 1950s—retires, beginning around the year 2010, there will be fewer workers per retired beneficiary than there are today. How will the liquidity of social security funds be maintained? As many economists have noted, in a pay-as-you-go system it is not a question of the system going "broke"; there are various measures that can assure adequate financing. Unfortunately, each of the measures gives rise to other problems.

The most obvious solution—the one already built into present legislation—calls for increasing payroll (or other) taxes.[5] But it is also obvious that this is not a popular measure and the burden of it is more likely to weigh heavily on those in the lower-income brackets than those in the higher brackets. In 1980, for example, the first $25,900 of earnings was subject to tax; thus, people in the lower-income brackets had a higher proportion of their income taxed than those who earned $26,000 or more.

Another measure that could be undertaken would be to reduce the level of retirement benefits. This clearly would not be a popular policy either. It would violate the expectations of retirees, a group whose growing size constitutes a formidable political force.

Still another possibility, either in combination with other proposals or as an alternative to them, is to raise the age of eligibility for benefits beyond age 65 (Sheppard & Rix, 1977). But this alternative runs counter to present trends where the majority of workers are retiring *before* age 65. It too is likely to meet resistance, especially from those who work in unpleasant jobs or harmful work environments and from those whose poor health is an incentive to retire early.

Whatever policies are adopted, they may run counter to the expectations of people who have come to view retirement as an earned right. Certain policies may cause hardships for prospective retirees. Thus, while the early cohorts of retirees may not have been prepared for life in retirement, future

---

[5]As of 1980, the first $25,900 of earnings was taxed at 6.13%. The rate is scheduled to go up to 6.65% in 1981 and to 6.70% in 1982–1984. Each employer and employee contributes these stated amounts that cover cash benefits for old age, survivors and disability insurance, and part of health insurance costs. Chapter 7 gives a more detailed description of social security benefits and regulations.

retirees may also not be ready for what awaits them. Because of the inexorability of social change, successive generations of retirees will face futures for which they are not or cannot be prepared. And such changes are bound to affect the individual and the way she or he feels about work and retirement. As you will see, the interplay between the individual and the society will be one of the recurrent themes in this book.

Plan of the Book

The major purpose of this book is to present an overview of retirement in American society. We will offer descriptive material about retirement and the problems associated with retirement, material we have culled from retirement research in the last several decades. At the same time, we search for explanations of these data. We wish to emphasize that our portrayal and explanations of the retirement process focus on people who have already retired or who are on the threshold of retirement. As we stress throughout the book, future cohorts of retirees and the social environment in which they will retire are likely to be quite different from those of the 1960s and 1970s. Thus, in interpreting data about retirement we are concerned not only with retirement as a key juncture in the aging process, but also with the impact of the succession of cohorts on the retirement process. In other words, we feel that retirement is a crucial transition in the life course and it is therefore necessary to look at various facets of the aging process—physiological, psychological, and social—as they affect retirement. It is also important to recognize that successive cohorts of retirees do not negotiate this transition in exactly the same way; the aging process itself is not immutable (Riley, 1978).

Following this chapter, we will first turn to questions about the capabilities of older workers. In Chapter 2 we consider whether retirement is a social necessity because older workers are incapable of meeting job requirements. Despite some widely held negative stereotypes, we will see that many older workers *are* fully able to meet job performance criteria.

Whatever the potential of older workers, a high proportion of older people in the United States are retired. In Chapter 3 we describe important characteristics of the retired population in the United States. The picture we present of retirees' financial status, health, marital status, activities, and residential concentration begins to suggest what retired life is like. Retirement appears to be characterized by both continuities with past practices in day-to-day living and losses in money, marital partners, and health.

Not only are a high proportion of older people presently retired, but there has been a trend toward **early retirement** (before age 65). In Chapter 4 we discuss this trend and whether it reflects pressures on older workers to leave their jobs or favorable attitudes toward retired life. We find both push and pull factors in the trend toward early retirement.

In Chapters 5 and 6 we explore life in retirement by examining the way retired people fill the retirement role, how they feel about life in retirement, and how individual characteristics and the family, community, and society affect life in retirement. In Chapter 7 we discuss some of the emerging society-wide problems associated with retirement: the financial squeeze—how to provide for increased pension costs—and the demographic squeeze—how to cope with fewer people of working age and increasing numbers of retirees—in the future.

In Chapter 8 we elaborate the theoretical perspective of our analysis. We discuss how age-related processes—aging and cohort succession—may affect retirees' reactions to retired life. We point to new problems and suggest that social change will inevitably give rise to new problems associated with retirement. Finally, we show how the interplay between the individual and the society affects the retirement role and serves to bring about further social change.

Throughout the book we suggest that there are many myths about retirement and older workers: for example, that older workers can't keep up or that retirement necessarily causes poor health and unhappiness. At the same time, we show that retirement is but one solution to a universal problem: how to manage the orderly replacement of individuals from one generation to the next to fill available social roles. And, we suggest that whatever the particular solution, it is likely to involve problems for the individual and the society. It will be the challenge of social policymakers to minimize these problems.

Review Questions
for Chapter 1

1. *What societal trends might stabilize or reverse the long-term trend toward declining labor force participation of older men?*
2. *Does the transition to retirement inevitably entail role discontinuities?*
3. *How has it been possible that everyone who has retired has received more than he or she put into the social security pension system?*
4. *Retirement concentrates leisure at the end of the life cycle. What are some of the other ways leisure could be distributed?*

Myths about Older Workers

A recurring issue in public and private decisions about work and retirement concerns the capabilities of older workers. Do they measure up? Should they be retired from the work force because they are not as competent as younger workers? Many people—even some older people themselves—believe so. Older people are thought to be less productive, slower, weaker, and less flexible on the job than younger people. Such views have wide repercussions: they can influence personnel decisions about hiring, firing, promotions, demotions, and transfers; they can sway public retirement policy; and they can affect older people's motivations. In this chapter we will examine just how widespread such stereotypes of older people are and scrutinize the accuracy of some stereotypes about the abilities of older people.

Stereotypes are widely held views about characteristics of a group. They are a shorthand way to judge members of particular groups. For example, some people have preconceptions about politicians, men and women, redheads, blacks, the Irish, Boy Scouts, and young or old people. We carry these judgments into our encounters with different categories of people. And some of these stereotypes are extremely inaccurate. Even when based on fact, no simple judgment can describe all members of a group equally well. In the case of older people, stereotypes based on misconceptions can unfairly limit opportunities. Inaccurate stereotypes can also influence older people's views of themselves and their capabilities.

Stereotypes about Older People

A 1974 national survey of Americans revealed that stereotypes of older people are indeed prevalent (Harris, 1975). The study explored a wide range of perceptions about older people, including characteristics that are relevant for job performance. Unlike many studies on the topic which have had to make do with small and/or nonrandom samples, the Harris study drew a large representative sample in order for its findings to be more reliably projected to the population of the United States. The study also included extra numbers of people 55 and over as well as of older black people so that these older people's attitudes could be more reliably measured than from a simple representative sample.

Table 2-1 shows a number of items from the Harris study that assess perceptions about older people's ability to work effectively at tasks and to relate well to other people. Comparing the percentages in columns A and B shows that people under 65 have strikingly different perceptions of older people than older people have of themselves. The largest differences occur in areas related to work: only 29% of people under 65 thought of most older people as "very bright and alert," while 68% of older people thought of themselves that way. Lack of "brightness" would presumably impinge upon a worker's ability to perform a job effectively.

Adaptability of workers is another valuable trait. In a technological society like ours, where continued experimentation and development of new techniques are considered keys to the goal of ever-increasing productivity, not being adaptable would be considered a critical deficiency in a worker. The largest differences in perceptions between the under-65 and over-65 sectors of the adult public occurred in the category "very open-minded and adaptable." Sixty-three percent of older sample members attributed this characteristic to themselves, but only 19% of younger sample members thought of older members of our society this way.

Still a third area of disagreement between the self-image of older people and the picture held by the younger public concerns the effectiveness of the elderly. Thirty-five percent of those under 65 thought older people were "very good at getting things done," whereas 55% of the older sample members themselves thought they were effective.

TABLE 2-1. *Perceptions of Older People Held by the Public, Self-Image of People 65 and Over, and Self-Image of People 18–64 Years of Age*

	Column A Image of "Most People Over 65" Held by Persons 18–64 %	Column B Self-Image of People 65 and Over %	Difference between A and B	Column C Self-Image of People 18–64 %	Difference between B and C
Very good at getting things done	35	55	−20	60	+ 5
Very open-minded and adaptable	19	63	−44	67	+ 4
Very bright and alert	29	68	−39	73	+ 5
Very physically active	41	48	− 7	65	+17
Very wise from experience	66	69	− 3	54	−15
Very friendly and warm	82	72	+10	63	− 9

Adapted from *The Myth and Reality of Aging in America*, by L. Harris and Associates. Copyright 1975 by National Council on the Aging, Inc. Reprinted by permission.

People both over and under 65 were in closer agreement about older people's physical activity. Less than half of younger sample members thought of the elderly as "very physically active" and about half of the older people thought of themselves in that way. Older persons' self-image and the younger public's view of the old were in close agreement on another trait— "very wise from experience." Although a positive stereotype, this image of the elderly might not be especially useful in helping them find employment. Since Americans often think of their productive system as highly technological and undergoing continuous development, traits of wisdom from previous experience may well be valued less highly than traits of adaptability and alertness. And as we have seen, the younger public rates the older population considerably lower on these traits than do older people themselves.

There is only one characteristic in the series that more younger persons attributed to the elderly than the elderly attributed to themselves. Eighty-two percent of the younger sample members said they thought of the elderly as "very friendly and warm." Such a view might be due to a kind of "grandparent halo"—that is, younger people in the society may have idealized views of what grandparents are like. They may have affectionate perceptions of their own grandparents and generalize about older people on this basis. Whatever the reason, the perception of older people as friendly and warm could be advantageous in some lines of work. For example, older people might be preferred to younger ones in programs that emphasize person-to-person contact rather than efficiency. Interestingly, a number of special programs of a volunteer or semivolunteer nature emphasize such interpersonal skills. The Foster Grandparent program, Gray Ladies, Senior Companions, Retired Senior Volunteer Program, and the special VISTA program for elderly volunteers are examples of programs that seem to try to capitalize on this special trait of the elderly.

In short, according to the Harris study, while most individuals 18–64 had some positive perceptions of older people, few adults under 65 thought that older people were very good at getting things done, very open-minded and adaptable, very bright and alert, or very physically active. Given this collection of stereotypes about older people, it is surprising that 59% of people 18–64 still felt that the elderly could continue to perform as well on the job as they did when they were younger. It is noteworthy that a majority of the under-65 adults have confidence in the performance capabilities of older workers. However, the fact that a substantial minority (about 40%) of under-65 adults believe that older workers' productivity declines with age, even on the jobs they have held for many years, can create serious obstacles for older workers. Further, the fact that negative stereotypes of older people are accepted by some older people themselves may discourage these older workers. (Note, however, that not all younger adults have positive self-images either. See column C, Table 2-1.)

Stereotypes about Older People Held
by Personnel Officers

Personnel officers' views about older workers' capabilities are particularly important. People who make hiring and other personnel decisions might hold opinions about the elderly that are quite different from those of the general public, since they come into contact with older workers and job seekers. If the views of personnel officers are more favorable than general public stereotypes, then the opportunities for older workers might be considerably better than is commonly assumed. The report on the Harris poll sometimes separated the replies of persons 18–64 who said they had responsibility on their jobs for hiring and firing people (21% of the sample 18–64).

On the series described in Table 2-1, the perceptions of "hirers and firers" were not reported separately for each item. But their summary score on these items (10.0) nearly duplicated that of the public at large (9.9). This finding indicates that people who hire and fire workers do *not* differ from the general public in their perceptions of older people. In fact, they were even less likely than the general public to believe that older workers can perform their jobs as capably as when they were younger (52% compared with 59% for all people 18–64 surveyed).

It seems likely that negative views of older people's capacities to work held by personnel officers (as well as by the public at large) limit older workers' opportunities for promotion, new jobs, and even the chance to keep their jobs. Some indirect evidence supports this. For example, a class exercise carried out among 142 students preparing to go into business careers showed that **agism** was indeed prevalent. In this study memos and letters described six different problems with an older or younger employee. The students were asked to read the description of the problem and then select one of several courses of action for dealing with it. The only variable manipulated in the experiment was the hypothetical employee's age. Each subject in the experiment received either the younger or older employee version of each experimental situation. For instance, one of the situations described "a computer programmer whose technical skills had become obsolete as a result of changes in computer operations" (Rosen & Jerdee, 1976, p. 429). The programmer was described as either 30 or 60 years old and of average ability. Participants evaluated the desirability of terminating the programmer and the desirability of retraining him.

In each of the six situations the students recommended different solutions for older than for younger employees. In the situation described above, subjects more often recommended termination for the older programmer and retraining for the younger programmer than any other solution. In the five other situations, the recommendations were also primarily to the *disadvantage* of the older workers. Of course, since this is a laboratory exercise, it may not reflect real-life situations. Further, the subjects, who were undergraduate students, may or may not typify the general population.

Other studies show that the findings of the business-student study are consistent with decisions made on the job. A 1965 study (this was before the 1967 **Age Discrimination in Employment Act**, which was designed to protect most workers aged 40–64) found that the reason cited most often by employers for setting up age hiring limits was the older workers' inability to meet the physical requirements of the job—one third of all reasons cited (Wirtz, 1965). According to Sheppard (1976), another reason for not hiring older workers is their lower educational levels. However, several studies reported by Sheppard suggest that age discrimination more than educational qualifications may be the underlying factor in hiring decisions. A 1962 study of 2000 hard-core unemployed in Detroit found that even when education, sex, race, and previous labor force participation were controlled in the analysis, age remained a significant factor in not employing older job applicants. And a study of unemployed engineers and scientists on the West Coast found that after controlling for technical competence and education, age was the most important factor explaining their layoffs from defense industries and that duration of joblessness was a function of age. There is as yet no systematic analysis of the impact of the Age Discrimination in Employment Act. It should also be noted that this legislation was amended in 1978 to provide protection to workers 65–69 and to move the permissible age for mandatory retirement from 65 to 70 for most workers.

Doubtless many factors enter into employers' decisions about training, layoffs, and hiring. Some employers believe that, compared with younger workers, older workers are more likely to become ill or disabled, will be more costly in fringe benefits like insurance or pensions, and that retraining will not pay off. But as Waring (1978) states, there is the problem of outright prejudice. General stereotypes of the old undoubtedly affect the decisions personnel officers make.

Evidence on the Accuracy of Stereotypes about the Old

We've already stated that stereotypes can be relatively accurate or they can be gross distortions of reality. One might argue that it is rational for an administrator to terminate older employees if they are indeed incapable of working effectively. Jacob Mincer (1968) has suggested that compulsory retirement at age 65 serves to simplify decisions about when to release older, less productive workers. But are older workers, in fact, less productive than younger workers? How does aging really affect the work capability of older people?

Below are several statements about characteristics of old people that can affect job performance and about which there is research evidence. Test your own preconceptions about older persons by indicating whether the statements in the following quiz are true or false.

1. Most people 65 and over suffer a mild to severe form of senility.
2. Most people lose muscular strength as they age and are unable to do heavy work as a consequence.
3. IQ declines in old age.
4. People 65 and over are slower at accomplishing tasks than younger people.
5. Most older workers are less productive than most workers under 65.

Stereotype 1: Most People 65 and Over Suffer a Mild to Severe Form of Senility

In popular usage the term *senility* calls to mind certain characteristics associated with old age. For example, an older person with a momentary lapse of memory may be called *senile*. *Webster's Third New International Dictionary* offers such synonyms as *decrepit, doddering, weak*. Actually, specialists in the field consider *senile dementia* to be a disease associated with distinct changes in the brain. Much remains to be learned about this affliction and much research is underway. According to current thinking, senility is viewed as a form of mental and neurological disorder that typically progresses from mild to severe impairment. In its early stages those suffering from senile dementia (most commonly older people) show "increased irritability, procrastination, loss of initiative, and difficulty in adapting to new situations and environment" (Shelanski, 1972, p. 114). At this stage of senility, the elderly person's difficulties may not even be apparent until or unless he or she experiences some major life change such as retirement or a geographical move. Gradually, the senile person experiences noticeable defects in memory of recent events while retaining memory of remote events. Many people at this stage of senile dementia die of other diseases like heart disease or cancer. If the patient survives this stage of recent memory impairment, he or she will usually "go on to a profound disorientation, social maladjustment, incontinence, and eventually coma and death" (Shelanski, 1972, p. 114).

The prevalence of senile brain disease among the elderly is difficult to estimate because of problems of diagnosis. For example, Butler (1975) has pointed out that any number of conditions can mock symptoms of senility and thus lead to overestimates of senile brain disorders. Severe depression, malnutrition, alcoholism, and undiagnosed physical ailments can all produce senile-like symptoms among the elderly. Alternatively, errors in clinical diagnosis often indicate the opposite: cases labeled cerebral arteriosclerosis are sometimes found on autopsy to be senile brain disease (Riley & Foner, 1968; see also Shelanski, 1972). Although doctors have grown increasingly sensitive to the difficulties of properly diagnosing senility, misdiagnosis is still a problem. While accurate diagnosis of senility by specialized physicians is difficult enough, designing standardized tests or interview protocols to be used by trained technicians who are not doctors is an even more formidable task (Ostfeld, 1972).

Problems of measurement and diagnosis aside, to the best of our current knowledge, rates of senile brain disease are not as high as commonly imagined. Estimates suggest that about 5%–15% of the population over 65 are suffering from senile brain disease or from some other clinically important mental impairment (Gilmore, 1974; Riley & Foner, 1968). It is not the case, then, that a high proportion of elderly persons fit the stereotype of being senile or mentally impaired.

Stereotype 2: Most People Lose Muscular Strength as They Age and, as a Consequence, Are Unable to Do Heavy Work

Another stereotype of older people is that they are frail and do not have strength or endurance to continue working. Research evidence on muscular strength does indicate that older people have less strength than younger people. For example, Welford's summary of four studies of handgrip strength (Welford, 1977) shows that strength is highest during the twenties and decreases thereafter with age. Three studies found persons aged 60–69 had about 80% of the handgrip strength of persons aged 20–29; one study found 60–69-year-old people had about 65% of the strength of 20–29-year-olds.

Another study (Shock & Norris, 1970) included shoulder static strength and shoulder cranking strength as well as handgrip strength measures. The subjects in these tests were 218 volunteers aged 20–89, well-educated and in good health. For one test subjects lay on their backs and turned a modified rear bicycle wheel with their hands. This measure of arm and shoulder strength produced results similar to those of handgrip strength. Adjusting for the weight differences between older and younger subjects produced somewhat smaller age differences. Interestingly, in their other measures of arm and shoulder strength, the researchers found less marked age differences. Indeed, in a different test, it was only some subjects over 60 who exhibited significantly less strength than younger subjects, with maximum differences occurring between those in their eighties and those under 60. When differences in body weight were taken into account, these age differences were reduced. The fact that different measures of strength yielded different age patterns indicates that strength is not a unitary concept. Age differences in strength may be more marked when coordination is involved (as in the bicycle test) than when static strength is measured.

It is important to emphasize here that the studies just described are based on **cross-sectional comparisons**. They compare older and younger people at a given time, and so it is misleading to make inferences from these data about how people change as they grow older. Older persons differ from younger ones not only in age but also in their lifetime experiences—for example, in their past nutrition patterns, their concern with exercise and self-care, their exposure to infectious diseases, and their susceptibility to chronic diseases. All of these factors might produce a lower average strength among older people as compared to younger people, quite apart from changes accompanying the aging process. Past nutrition practices, for example, may help account for the fact that older people, on the average, are shorter and weigh less than younger people. On the basis of their smaller size alone, we might expect older people to exhibit less strength than younger people.

Alternatively, there are other factors that may put older people at an advantage over younger people in tests of strength. First, older people are *survivors*. That is, some of the less healthy members of the cohort died before reaching the later years, thus leaving what may be a relatively healthy and perhaps relatively strong group of people to perform strength tests. Second, technological developments have reduced the strength required in many jobs, which means that the average younger person may have had less muscular exercise on the job than the average older person. A lifetime of such physical exercise may contribute to maintenance of physical strength in older workers.

Ideally, then, we need studies that take these several factors into consideration. For example, **longitudinal studies** of several cohorts can trace changes that occur in the same individuals as they grow older *and* can also show whether these changes with aging are the same for several cohorts having different lifetime experiences. Further, both cross-sectional and longitudinal studies should consider the effects of such variables as occupation, health, and body weight on measures of strength.

In the absence of studies that fit the ideal design, it is difficult to pinpoint the sources of age differences in strength that have been observed. However, a few studies that go beyond simple cross-section comparisons are of interest. First, recall that when researchers held body weight constant in their analysis, cross-section age differences in measured strength were lower than without such controls. One implication of this finding is that cohort differences in size contribute to the relatively lower strength of older people. Second, a longitudinal study of a small sample of French men and women is suggestive. Over a period of five to ten years, there was an average decline in strength among sample members—a finding that supports the assumption that some decline in strength occurs as people grow older (Clement, 1974).

In summary, available research indicates that older people exhibit less strength than younger people on a variety of tests of muscular strength. But this hardly means that older workers should be barred from most jobs. It is untenable to overgeneralize about older people's loss of strength. In the first place, many jobs in our society require little heavy work. Even on jobs requiring some physical strength, many older people do extremely well. The data described above refer to averages; actually there are enormous individual differences, and relatively few older people show extreme decrements in strength. Moreover, the critical age when differences in strength appear varies with the type of strength measured. Further, people may learn how to maximize their strength in the later years by reserving top capacity for special occasions, interspersing effort with rest periods, and generally working at a slower pace (Troll, 1975). In addition, there is some evidence that exercise can not only help maintain power but may even increase muscular strength (Skinner, 1969).

Finally, we must be careful about making predictions about the capabilities of older people of the future. Oncoming generations of old people won't necessarily be the same as people who are old now.

Stereotype 3: Intelligence Declines with Age

The negative stereotype of the old as victims of declining intelligence is one of the most pervasive and durable beliefs about aging. Recall that in the Harris poll only 29% of the general public under 65 thought of the old as "very bright and alert." Such beliefs are based on what many people thought was scientific evidence. Researchers had been looking at the intellectual performance of people of different ages at the same point in time and had concluded from these cross-section studies that there was a decline in intelligence in people as they aged. As we now have come to understand, such inferences from cross-section data about changes over the individual's life course can be misleading and inaccurate.

Cross-Section Studies. Early cross-section studies of intelligence found that overall scores on tests of intelligence peaked in adolescence and then declined with age thereafter. More recent cross-section studies of intellectual performance showed somewhat similar results, but found that scores increase with age up to early adulthood (age 30 or so) and decline with age thereafter (Barton, Plemons, Willis, & Baltes, 1975).

Comparisons of younger and older people on overall test scores, however, can be misleading. Intelligence tests include measures of different kinds of intellectual abilities. Because many existing intelligence tests have been constructed with a primary focus on the young, some scholars wonder whether intelligence tests neglect abilities—wisdom, for example—that are salient in the adult and later years (Baltes, Reese, & Lipsitt, 1980). But even on existing tests, when subjects are given separate scores for different components of intelligence, the age patterns are not consistent. For example, one distinction that is frequently made is between verbal and nonverbal abilities. Age differences on verbal tests—like tests of information and vocabulary—are less marked than age differences on nonverbal tests—like picture completion tests that involve psychomotor functions and often emphasize speed. Thus, once researchers show separate scores for the many dimensions of intellectual functioning, cross-section studies do not indicate that younger people's performance is uniformly superior to that of older people.

Longitudinal Studies.   Important as cross-section findings are, they do not tell us whether intelligence declines as individuals grow older. We cannot assume that age differences observed at one time mean changes with aging. It is not surprising therefore that longitudinal studies (typically following members of a single cohort) produce results that differ from cross-section studies. When the same individuals are measured periodically over a period of time, intellectual performance remains stable or even increases well into the fifties (Schaie, 1979; Barton et al., 1975). Some longitudinal studies of persons over 60 show some decline in intellectual functioning, but not as great as the decline with age seen in the cross-section studies (Riley & Foner, 1968; Botwinick, 1977).

Further, once different components of intellectual abilities are considered, no uniform pattern of change with aging is noted in longitudinal studies. One longitudinal study found that in several different age cohorts there was no decline with aging over a seven-year period in some components of intellectual functioning, and an increment in performance in others, even in the oldest group—those going from age 70 to age 77 (Baltes & Schaie, 1974). The study measured four different dimensions of intellectual functioning: crystallized intelligence, which consists of skills acquired through education, experience, and acculturation, as in tests of verbal comprehension or semantic relations; cognitive flexibility, the ability to shift from one way of thinking to another, as with synonyms and antonyms; visuo-motor flexibility, the ability to shift from familiar to unfamiliar patterns in visuo-motor tasks, as when one copies words but interchanges capital with lower-case letters; and visualization, the ability to organize and process visual materials, as finding a simple figure in a complex one. This study did not contain sufficient measures of fluid intelligence, which involves organizing and reorganizing information in the process of solving problems (Baltes & Schaie, 1974). The researchers found a decline with aging only in visuo-motor flexibility; scores of crystallized intelligence and visualization actually showed improvement with aging. A 14-year follow-up of this sample and a seven-year longitudinal study of an independent sample support the general finding that decrements in many components of intellectual functioning do not set in until advanced old age (Schaie, 1979).

One reason longitudinal studies show little decline in IQ test scores appears to be the selective dropout of participants in longitudinal research. For various reasons people who perform poorly tend to be less available for longitudinal retesting than people who perform well. Thus, the respondents who remain in these studies tend to be superior performing subjects (Botwinick, 1977; Schaie, 1979).

Cohort Differences. Differing results of longitudinal and cross-section studies are due not only to sample attrition in longitudinal research but also to marked differences between cohorts in performance on intelligence tests. People of different ages observed at one time period, as in cross-section research, are members of different birth cohorts. Each cohort has been exposed to different environmental forces that, in turn, can affect performance on IQ tests. In fact, such **cohort differences** were observed in the study just described. Because several cohorts were followed over a seven-year period, researchers could make two types of comparisons. They could measure changes with aging by looking at the performances of individuals in 1956 and then measure the same individuals seven years later in 1963—for example, people going from 25 in 1956 to 32 in 1963 or going from 53 to 60. They could also compare people from different cohorts at the same age by comparing, for example, subjects who were 53 in 1956 with different subjects who were 53 in 1963 or those who were 32 in 1956 with others who were 32 in 1963. The researchers found that much of the difference in intellectual performance between young and old was not due to a decline in ability among the old but was related to the higher performance levels in successive cohorts (Baltes & Schaie, 1974). Similar cohort differences were found in a 14-year follow-up (Schaie et al., 1973).

Several factors may account for the increases in measured intelligence among successively younger cohorts. A major factor is the substance, method, and length of education received by members of each cohort. Level of education is associated with performance on intelligence tests and younger people have had more education than older people. In addition, younger adults have had more recent education and their education is likely to be more applicable to IQ tests than the education older people received. Younger people also have had more experience taking tests than older people. It has also been suggested that dramatic changes in the quality and delivery of health care may be related to cohort differences in performance on IQ tests. For example, prenatal and perinatal medical care may have an impact on later intellectual functioning (Barton et al., 1975). Improvements in such medical care would benefit more recent (and therefore younger) cohorts.

Variations among Older People. Older individuals are, of course, not all alike; they vary in their abilities as do individuals of any age. Thus, some older people maintain their former IQ levels, others show some decline, while still others gain in certain types of intellectual performance as they grow older. One of the tasks researchers are now beginning to undertake is to explore why some individuals maintain intellectual functioning better in old age than do others (Jarvik, 1975). Preliminary research has found, for example, that nearness to death may bring about a decline in intellectual functioning; there is some indication of a "terminal drop" in intelligence scores in the last year or so of life (possibly in the last four or five years). Women seem to decline at a slower rate than men, but this may be due to the greater longevity of women or to test biases (Jarvik, 1975; Riegel & Riegel, 1972). Finally, some researchers suggest that training or heightened motivation may improve intellectual performance (Baltes & Schaie, 1974; Baltes & Willis, 1979).

In other words, careful research has contradicted the commonly held view that intelligence uniformly declines with aging. Older people may not do as well as younger people in cross-section studies of intellectual performance—at least in their total scores on IQ tests—but longitudinal analysis indicates that several types of intellectual development may continue well into the later years. In addition, there is variation among the old in the maintenance of intelligence in later life. And the declines that have been observed among the old are not nearly as marked as was once believed.

Stereotype 4: Older People Are Slower than Younger People

Experimental evidence indicates that older people's reaction time is slower than that of younger people. *Reaction time* is defined as the time between a signal and the beginning of the subject's response to that signal. For example, when subjects have been tested for simple reaction time—as pressing a key in response to sound or a light or brake reaction time—studies have consistently demonstrated that there is a small but definite increase in reaction time with age (Riley & Foner, 1968). Age differences in reaction time appear to be independent of the sensory organ stimulated and the type of response measured (Botwinick, 1973). It is unclear whether making the task more difficult—as in increasing the number of alternative signal sources, increasing the complexity of sorting tasks, increasing the number of choices to be made—produces a disproportionate increase in the reaction time of older subjects.

Although in almost every study, the old are seen as slower than the young, individual differences among the old are great. In fact, the range of individual differences is larger for the old than for the young, and many old people are faster than young people. Further, research indicates that several factors can increase the speed of response of older subjects. Practice and experience can reduce age differences and possibly eliminate them. Regular physical exercise and heightened motivation may also quicken response time in older people (Botwinick, 1973). Finally, we do not know why or how speed of response changes with aging in certain individuals and if or how the relatively slow reaction time of older people affects their performance outside the laboratory.

Stereotype 5: Older Workers Are Less
Productive than Younger Workers

Thus far we have shown that some stereotypes of the old are incorrect—the vast majority of older people do not become senile, and there is little inevitable decline in intellectual functioning. We have also suggested that many differences between young and old that have been observed in cross-section studies are not marked. Further, there is wide variation among old people. For example, some old people achieve higher scores on intelligence tests than other older people and some younger people. Nevertheless, comparisons of young and old at one point in time do show that, on the average, older people have less muscular strength, are slower, and do not perform as well on some types of intelligence tests as younger people. The questions that need to be asked next are: What is the effect of these age differences on the productivity and creativity of older workers? Does the work performance of older workers suffer? Are older workers able to compensate for whatever disadvantages they do experience?

Most of the studies we have discussed in this chapter have included both working and nonworking old people in their study populations. And that is appropriate for research questions about age differences and changes associated with aging. But it is not appropriate for questions about older *workers*. Workers who experience a severe decline in their abilities to carry out specific tasks are likely to leave the labor force, either voluntarily or with a strong shove from their employers. Older persons who remain in the labor force are probably a select group for that reason—on the average, they are probably somewhat healthier and more competent than their age-mates out of the labor force.

The studies on job performance reviewed below are all cross-section studies that compare older and younger workers in a variety of work settings. These studies indicate that age patterns in average rates of productivity (output or sales) vary depending on the type of work involved. For example:

- There was a slight decline at age 60 + in output per hour among 6000 mail sorters in the U.S. post office (Walker, 1964).
- There was some decline in sales performance beyond a peak in the fifties among 1000 retail sales clerks in two large urban Canadian department stores (Canadian Department of Labor, 1959).
- There were no significant age differences in output among 6000 clerical workers in five federal agencies and 21 private companies (U.S. Bureau of Labor Statistics, 1960).
- There were declines in output (beyond a peak in the middle years) among 5000 incentive factory workers in 22 manufacturing firms in the furniture and footwear industries (Mark, 1957).

The older worker's greater experience on the job may contribute to the relatively high output rates observed in various studies. However, even when experience is held constant, the output rates of older workers continued to approximate that of younger workers among the office workers, postal employees, and retail sales personnel noted above. A more recent, small study of a random sample of production workers on a standard time, piece-rate pay system found that there were no significant age differences in productivity after differences in experience were taken into account (Schwab & Heneman, 1977).

In certain other aspects of job performance, older workers are found to be as good as or better than younger workers. For example, older mail sorters and office workers performed at steadier rates from week to week than younger workers did. Older workers have been found to maintain the same quality of work as younger workers. In a study of 18,000 workers in over 100 manufacturing plants and 9000 production workers in furniture and footwear establishments, attendance rates of older workers were found to be approximately the same as those of younger workers. And older workers are more committed to the work they do than are younger workers (Riley & Foner, 1968).

Finally, a special kind of productivity—creative productivity—appears to be maintained by older scientists, artists, and scholars in many fields. Classic examples of creativity in the later years are well known. Grandma Moses, for example, began painting at age 76 and continued painting into the last year of her life. She painted 25 pictures after reaching 100 years of age. Igor Stravinsky composed *Requiem Canticles* when he was 84. G. Stanley Hall, a psychologist who influenced educational psychology, published his book *Senescence* at 78.

Are these examples rare exceptions? Apparently not. When the full life curve of productivity among those living into old age is examined, marked declines in old age occur only in certain types of creative activity. Historical, philosophical, and literary scholarship is maintained at a fairly stable level into old age. There are moderate declines in the sciences (with the exception of botany, which shows smallest drops). In the arts, productivity declines more sharply, particularly among dramatists, architects, and librettists. However, even where there is a general decline in creative output with aging, older people often do a considerable part of their total work in their later years. The decade from age 70 to 79 alone accounts for 20% of the output in the fields of scholarship, 15% in the sciences, and 6% in the arts (Dennis, 1966).

A recent analysis of the performance of mathematicians over a 25-year period is of particular interest because mathematicians have been thought to peak quite early. Among a cohort of mathematicians receiving their Ph.D. degrees in the period 1947–1950, patterns of scientific productivity established early in their careers were maintained as the mathematicians grew older. People who began their careers by publishing and were recognized for making important contributions generally continued to publish high-quality work over the 25-year period covered in the study. Some of the most widely cited papers were produced 20–25 years after the Ph.D. was received (Cole, 1979).

Conclusion

The stereotype of the older worker as less capable than the younger worker is partially based upon fact and partially upon myth: that is the trouble with stereotypes. They are half-truths that can be more harmful than outright lies because they have "an aura of plausibility concealing their untruth" (Rhinelander, 1977–1978, p. 2). The most serious effect of stereotypes is that people are not judged on their own merits.

Although there may be some truth in each of the stereotypes we have reviewed, we have shown that each stereotype overgeneralizes and oversimplifies. True, older people may be at a disadvantage when compared to younger people in some attributes relevant to job performance; but older workers are as good as or better than younger workers in other job-related characteristics. Further, there is substantial variation in the capacities of older people: even the same individual may do better at certain types of tasks than on others; some old people perform more competently than others, and some even have qualifications that are superior to those of younger persons. Moreover, age differences between the young and old that have been observed are often not large. Thus, evidence does not justify the automatic exclusion of older people from their jobs on the basis of their qualifications; there is too much variation in talents in old age and in the skills called for in jobs to warrant any arbitrary judgments based solely on age.

Perhaps it is not accidental that in this era of mass retirement negative stereotypes about older people's capabilities are common. These exaggerated stereotypes about the old may perform a function for society. Negative stereotypes about the old facilitate the difficult decisions many employers face in hiring or releasing older workers; such stereotypes help to legitimate the exclusion of older workers from the labor force. On their part, older workers themselves, believing that age brings about a decline in capacities and in health, may well have accepted the idea of retirement more easily.

If these speculations are correct, then the coming difficulties of financing retirement may encourage the development of new perceptions about older workers. Instead of an emphasis on the inability of older people to work, new images may emerge to highlight older workers' competence or even superiority. A general belief that older people should work might result in hardships for some, just as today's stereotypes about the old may keep competent older persons out of the labor force.

Review Questions
for Chapter 2

1. *How do you account for negative stereotypes of older people held by adults under 65? What might be some of the reasons negative stereotypes*

about aged workers continue to prevail even though research has shown many such stereotypes to be misleading?

2. What are the limitations of cross-section studies in analyzing the aging process? Do longitudinal studies overcome all these limitations?

3. How might changes in the social environment affect the physiological processes of aging and the capabilities of older workers?

4. What do data based on average performance or average physiological functioning tell us about the capabilities of individual older workers?

5. The entry of more women into the labor force might increase the difficulties some older workers have in locating new jobs. Why might that be the case?

3

A Profile
of the
Retired
Population

Regardless of the potential abilities of older workers, the trend in this century, at least up to 1980, has been for increasingly higher proportions of older workers to retire from the labor force. What, then, is retirement like? For many reasons—gaps in research, variations among retirees—there is no simple answer to this question. A first step in understanding the nature of retirement in contemporary American society and the problems associated with it is to illustrate what retired people are like. In this chapter we will describe some important characteristics of retired people in the 1970s: their financial situations, where they live, and what they do now that they are no longer working. In reviewing data on these aspects of retirees' lives, we are aware that the picture we present may change even within the next decade; for some of today's retirees will die and new retirees with different characteristics and life histories will enter the picture and these new retirees, in turn, will be retiring in a new social and economic environment. Nevertheless, our description suggests the parameters influencing the retirees and the lives they make for themselves.

Describing the current population of retired persons might seem a simple task, but it is not. There is no single agreed-upon definition of what retirement is. So far, we have tended to equate retirement with withdrawal from the labor force, but this is not the definition used by all researchers in collecting all data. We will note which definition is used where such information is provided.

Among the definitions that have been used are the following: a reduction in hours worked, a reduction in work responsibilities, nonparticipation in the labor force, receipt of social security benefits, receipt of private pensions, and definition of oneself as retired. These alternative definitions are likely to refer to different groups of retirees. For example, police officers or members of the armed forces might retire from their duties and receive pensions, but then go on to other jobs. According to one definition—receipt of private or public pensions—they would be retired; but according to another—nonparticipation in the labor force—they would not be retired.

The most commonly used definitions are labor force status, receipt of social security benefits, and definition of oneself as retired. Research has begun to sort out the results of using one definition over another. Irelan and Bell (1972) analyzed a subgroup of respondents who were part of a larger, longitudinal study conducted by the Social Security Administration. They found that most people who defined themselves as "completely retired" in 1969 were out of the labor force—that is, neither working nor looking for work. Those who said they were "not retired at all" generally participated in the labor force. This research implies that at least for these respondents, labor force status and self-defined retirement were closely linked.

Problems of definition aside, there is a considerable accumulation of data about the retired population or selected segments of the retired population in the United States. In the following pages we draw on these materials to review the financial status, health, marital status, residence, and activities of retirees in the 1970s.

Age at Retirement

Ever since social security legislation was passed in 1935, it has become customary to think of age 65 as the magic number, signaling the time at which most individuals withdraw from the labor force. Actually, most of today's retirees retired before they were 65. A 1978 national survey found that almost two-thirds of the retired employees (defined as no longer in full-time employment) reported that they had retired before age 65; one-fifth had retired before they were 55; 22% had retired at age 65. The median age of retirement in this sample was 60.6 (Harris, 1979). By the definition of retirement used in this survey, some of the people considered retired might have gone on to other jobs. At the time of the survey, however, 81% were not employed; 5% said they were housewives; 8% were employed part-time, and 5% were employed full-time. These data about early retirement are generally consistent with labor force statistics that indicate a trend toward early retirement, something we will discuss more fully in Chapter 4.

The fact that many people have retired before age 65 can be attributed in part to social security regulations that permit workers covered by social security to retire between ages 62 and 65 at benefits somewhat lower than what would have been available had the worker remained in the labor force until age 65. If these regulations are modified—and, as we discuss in Chapter 7, proposals for such modifications have been put forward—the trend toward early retirement may be reversed.

Financial Status

Retirees generally have to make do with relatively low incomes—lower than the incomes they had when they were working. Although the average income of retirees has improved in the 1970s, many retirees still live on small pensions or social security benefits and do not have other economic resources.

In 1976, for example, the median income of "aged units" (either a married couple in which at least one member was 65 or over, or a nonmarried person 65 or over) receiving any type of social security benefit was only $4680 (Grad & Foster, 1979). These "aged units" include a minority of older people who are not, strictly speaking, retirees—for example, wives of deceased workers who receive **survivor benefits** but who have not had paid employment themselves, or individuals who may not consider themselves retired because they work at jobs, albeit with small yearly earnings. By the same token, the average income noted above excludes people receiving retired-worker or disability benefits who are under age 65.

Is this average income of retirees really low? Relatively speaking, it is. Consider the following:

- The median income of slightly younger people is considerably higher than that of retirees. Individuals and couples aged 55–61 in 1976 who were not receiving social security benefits—presumably because they or their spouses were in the labor force—had a median income of $13,260. This is more than double the income of retirees and other recipients of social security benefits who were 65 and over (Grad & Foster, 1979).
- Retirees have lower incomes than employed people of the same age. For example, in 1972, among married men who were then age 62–66 and their spouses, 51% of those who were employed had incomes of $10,000 a year or more compared with 20% of those who had retired since 1968 and 9% of those who had retired before 1968. As Table 3-1 shows, the same pattern of relatively low incomes among the retired holds for nonmarried men and women.
- Retirement is accompanied by a sharp drop in income. According to recent longitudinal data, for example, couples who retired in 1973–1974 had a median **replacement rate** of 55%. In other words, pension and social security income received by the average couple replace just over half of their preretirement income (A. Fox, 1979).

TABLE 3-1. Income of Employed and Retired People Aged 61–66 in 1972

Total Money Income 1972	Employed in 1972 %	Employed in 1968 but Not in 1972 %	Not Employed in 1968 or 1972 %
Married men and spouses			
Less than $2500	4	12	18
$2500–$4999	13	25	34
$5000–$9999	33	44	39
$10,000 or more	51	20	9
Nonmarried men			
Less than $2500	12	31	53
$2500–$4999	22	43	30
$5000–$9999	38	22	12
$10,000 or more	29	4	5
Nonmarried women			
Less than $2500	16	52	71
$2500–$4999	31	28	22
$5000–$9999	39	16	5
$10,000 or more	14	3	1

Adapted from A. Fox, 1976, pp. 19–20.

Some retirees have such low incomes that they have to depend on public assistance to survive. In 1976, 10% of social security beneficiaries 65 and over received public assistance of some sort, usually Supplementary Security Income or **SSI**—income supplements to certain older people with very low incomes (Grad & Foster, 1979). Such SSI recipients were more likely than other aged beneficiaries to be black, widowed, and have had less than an eighth-grade education (Sally R. Sherman, 1979). Programs such as SSI and Medicare (which pays a share of older people's medical costs) have helped ease the plight of poor older people.

It is also noteworthy that the proportion of poor older people seems to have been reduced over time. In 1959, 27% of older people living in families were below the **poverty level**, as measured by federal agencies; by 1977, only 8% were classified as poor. For older people living alone or with nonrelatives, the change in the proportion who were poor also declined from 62% in 1959 to 27% in 1977. Although the proportion of younger people in poverty also declined, the decline was not as dramatic (U.S. Bureau of the Census, 1979b).

Sources of Income

Social security benefits are the mainstay of retirees' incomes, but they are not intended to replace the retiree's entire former income. Rather, the benefits are meant to provide a foundation of economic support. In 1976, beneficiaries 65 and over received a **median income** of $2870 from social security (Grad & Foster, 1979).

Fortunately for some retirees, they have other sources of income. Pensions other than social security are among the most important of these other income sources. Indeed, retirees with a private or public pension in addition to social security generally have higher incomes than those without second pensions (A. Fox, 1976). Retirees with second pensions tend to have had higher earnings while working than retirees without second pensions. And once they retire, their retirement incomes replace a higher proportion of their preretirement incomes than the proportion replaced among those with only social security benefits (A. Fox, 1976). Retirement was defined in this analysis as stopping paid employment.

But only about half the workers are covered by private pensions (Yohalem, 1977). Where there is such coverage, it is not distributed randomly throughout the working population. For example, men are more likely to be covered than women, primarily because men have the kinds of jobs that are covered by private pensions. Professionals have highest rates of coverage while sales workers, laborers, service workers, and farm workers have the lowest. Further, a substantial number of private workers who have worked in employment covered by private pension plans do not receive pension benefits when they retire (G. B. Thompson, 1978a). Lack of *vested rights* (**vesting** refers to acquisition of full legal title to the benefits made possible by the employer's contribution to a pension plan),[1] withdrawal of employee contributions upon termination of employment, and bankruptcy of the business or its pension plan are some of the major factors accounting for the nonreceipt of pension benefits. Only 31% of aged beneficiary units in 1976 are reported to have actually received second pensions. These recipients of private pensions or annuities received a median amount of $1860 for the year (Grad & Foster, 1979). One other problem is that private pension benefits have generally not increased to meet rising prices during inflationary times, unlike social security benefits, which are geared to rising prices.

Another potential source of income to retirees is assets—for example, income from savings in the bank or from stocks and bonds. Many retirees do have the security of owning their own homes with little or no mortgage debt. However, few individuals reach retirement age with sufficient assets to provide

[1]Before legislation went into effect in 1976, employees often did not acquire a right to the benefits made possible by the employer's contribution to a private pension plan until they were close to retirement age, no matter how many years of service they may have had. There were individuals who had worked as long as 30 years for a company but still had not qualified for a pension. The new legislation made this illegal. The **Employee Retirement Income Security Act (ERISA)** requires all employers who voluntarily set up private pension plans that qualify for tax privileges to make every employee working at least 1000 hours a year who is at least 25 years of age (unless he or she was hired within five years of normal retirement age) and who has completed at least one year of service, eligible for vested benefit rights. The amount of vesting depends on the years of employment with the employer and, to some extent, on the employee's age (O'Meara, 1977).

supplementary income (Sally R. Sherman, 1976). Of aged couples or individuals receiving some type of social security benefits, 57% reported some income from assets. But this type of income tends to be low. For aged units (both beneficiaries and nonbeneficiaries of social security) with some income from assets, the median amount in 1976 was only $870 (Grad & Foster, 1979).

Finally, it should be noted that some people who receive social security benefits have earnings from part-time or full-time employment. As of 1980, retired workers 65 and over might earn $5000 a year and still qualify for full social security benefits. The annual exemption is scheduled to go up to $6000 by 1982. Workers 72 and over are presently exempt from all earnings restrictions and the new law specifies that by 1982 persons 70 and over will be entitled to such an exemption. In 1976, just one-quarter of aged beneficiary units 65 and over reported job earnings; the median amount of these earnings was $2530, quite close to the annual exemption of $2760 at that time (Grad & Foster, 1979).

Variations among Retirees

As the data we have reviewed make clear, retirees vary in their financial situations. Blacks tend to be one of the most disadvantaged groups. The typical black worker earns less than the typical white worker; as a result, social security benefits of blacks are, on the average, lower than those of whites. For example, among individuals newly eligible for **retired-worker benefits** from social security between July 1968 and June 1970, 70% of the black men, compared to 40% of the white men, had **Primary Insurance Amounts** (PIAs) below $150 a month. (The Primary Insurance Amount is the benefit level an individual can receive from social security if he or she retires at age 65.) The corresponding figures for black and white women were 90% and 75%. As noted above, most individuals retire before age 65 and receive less than their Primary Insurance Amount. Blacks also receive second pensions less frequently than whites. Among all people receiving retired-worker benefits from social security, 18% of the black men and 35% of the white men received or expected second pensions; the figures for black and white women were 7% and 18% respectively (Rubin, 1976).

Women are also relatively disadvantaged. We have already stated that women are less likely than men to have second pension coverage. If they do have such coverage in private employment, they are less likely than men to actually receive benefits when they retire. Women typically have earned less in their working years than men; thus, they are more likely than men to have low PIAs. Some women receiving social security benefits are widows who did not work long enough to qualify for pensions and social security on their own work records and must rely on survivor benefits. On the average, survivor benefits are lower than benefits paid to retired or disabled workers (*Social Security Bulletin,* 1979).

Still another important sector of the retired population, people who have been retired a long time—usually the more elderly members of the retired population—are also at a disadvantage. People who retired many years ago worked in periods when income levels were lower than they are now. Since social security benefits are tied to a certain extent to the individual's earnings record, the social security benefits of these long-time retirees are lower than the benefits of those retiring more recently. In addition, long-time retirees are less likely than recent retirees to be covered by second pensions (A. Fox, 1976).

As you can see, some retirees do fairly well in retirement while others have a difficult time making do. Retirees who are able to combine several sources of retirement income stand a better chance of having an adequate income. People who had better paying jobs when they were working are not only more likely to have second pension coverage, but also to have higher social security benefits than those who had low- and moderate-paying jobs. For those with low incomes in retirement—disproportionately blacks, women, single persons, and people with low educational attainment—making ends meet is often a struggle. But even for many of the more fortunate retirees, retirement is a less than affluent time of life. As we shall see in Chapter 5, the adequacy of retirement income is an important influence on the way retirees fit into the retirement role.

Health

As people grow older, they are more likely to have chronic illnesses than when they were younger, so it is not surprising to find that many retirees are not in good health. According to their self-reports, retirees have many health problems. The Retirement History Study conducted by the Social Security Administration asked respondents: "Does your health limit the kind or amount of work you can do?" Among those who had been working in 1969 but had stopped working by 1973 when they were 62–67 years old, half the sample said they had health problems sufficiently serious to interfere with their ability to work. Thirty percent of the sample reported that their health prevented them from working at all (Motley, 1978). However, self-reports can produce some misreporting, as some respondents will try to minimize health problems and others will exaggerate or invent them. Some of the "unhealthy" retirees may say they have health problems because they feel that poor health is the only justifiable reason for not working. In any event, most old people have no criteria by which to assess their own health.

All such problems aside, according to some small studies there is a correlation between self-reported health status and other methods of assessing health, such as physicians' ratings (Riley & Foner, 1968). And, on balance, there appears to be a substantial number of retirees with health limitations. We will discuss problems of interpreting self-reported health status more fully in Chapter 4.

Retirees face not only loss in income and deterioration of health but also the death of a spouse. Whether or not a retired person is married has implications for her or his well-being. As we discuss in Chapter 6, retirees who have had their marriage break up because of death or divorce appear to be at a disadvantage in retirement; they lack an important source of **social support.**

Recent information on the marital status of the entire retired population is not available, but we do have data on the marital status of people beginning to collect retired-worker benefits from the social security program who retired from July to December 1968. As shown in Table 3-2, most people beginning to collect benefits were married. But a sizable minority of the women were widowed, and some were separated or divorced. Since women live longer than men and tend to marry husbands older than themselves, more women than men are widowed.

TABLE 3-2.   *Marital Status of Newly Entitled Retired-Worker Beneficiaries, July–December 1968*

Marital Status	Men %	Women %
Married	78	62
Nonmarried	22	38
Widowed	7	20
Divorced or separated	7	9
Never married	7	8
Not specified	2	2
Number	196,000	175,000

Adapted from Lauriat & Rabin, 1976, p. 14.

It is important to emphasize that these data refer to people who were starting to collect benefits and were, therefore, relatively young, on the average, compared to retirees as a whole. We can get some idea of the marital status

TABLE 3-3.   *Marital Status of Population 65 and Over by Age and Sex, 1978*

Marital Status	Men 65–74 %	Men 75+ %	Women 65–74 %	Women 75+ %
Single	5.7	4.8	6.6	5.7
Married	81.1	70.4	48.3	22.9
Widowed	9.7	23.0	41.2	69.3
Divorced	3.5	1.8	3.9	2.1

Based on U.S. Bureau of the Census, 1979b, p. 42.

of retirees as a whole by looking at the marital status of all people 65 and over. Table 3-3 shows the distribution of the U.S. population 65 and over by marital status in 1978. At that time only 48% of the women 65–74 were married and 41% were widowed. Much higher proportions of men were married and fewer were widowed. Among both men and women 75 and over, the proportion of widowed individuals is considerably higher than among those between the ages of 65 and 74.

The human side of these data is clear. Cut off from daily contact with coworkers and facing retired life without a spouse, often living alone, many retired persons will have to deal with problems of loneliness in their retirement years.

Activities in Retirement

Apart from concerns with retirees' financial, health, and marital status, a major focus of interest in the lives of retirees is the additional time they have on their hands. Most employed adults spend much of their time working, commuting to and from work, preparing for work, and perhaps talking about work after hours. What do retirees do with these extra hours? Some people worry that retirees might "waste" their time if not properly directed, or that they will be bored or deteriorate with so much free time.

One alternative is for retirees to reduce activities and social involvements. Some researchers have theorized that individuals generally disengage from activities as they age. Cumming and Henry (1961) found that in a small sample the older the individual, the lower her or his overall level of activity, on the average. However, they included work as part of the overall activity score for sample members, and, since nearly all men retire from work as they age, such a measure of activity levels automatically shows a decline with age and does not permit us to assess activity levels in retirement per se.

Another option for retirees is to seek out activities that can substitute for the work role. Some people believe that retirement produces a void in the lives of individuals, not only in terms of time but also in terms of the individual's sense of worth. They expect retirees will increase the time they spend in nonwork activities in order to fill this void and to feel useful and worthwhile—for example, engage in grandparenting, voluntary participation, or hobbies.

Yet a third approach is for retirees to maintain fairly consistent levels of activities before and after retirement. They neither disengage from, step up, nor start new kinds of activities. Rather they tend to maintain familiar patterns of activity.

Data from the Retirement History Study allow us to examine the activity levels of a large, nationally representative sample of individuals before and after retirement. In 1971 sample members were 60–65 years old. In 1975 they were 64–69 years old, and many had stopped working. The 1975 wave of interviews asked respondents to report the frequency with which they engaged in a large number of different activities. For example, respondents were asked about the frequency of their television viewing. The interviewers noted whether respondents reported watching television daily, weekly, monthly, less than monthly, or not at all. Respondents were then asked a series of parallel questions about their activities five years previously. These data allow us to compare the activity levels of individuals in retirement with what they perceived their activity levels to be prior to retirement.

Of course, some changes in activity might be due to aging or cohort differences rather than retirement. Individuals might decrease their involvement in sports activities, for example, because they are older and not because they retired. In order to examine this cause of activity changes, respondents who had not retired over that time interval were also studied.

Table 3-4 compares the activity patterns of respondents who had stopped working after 1971 with those who continued to work. If respondents reported they watched TV weekly five years previously, but daily at the present time, their TV viewing was considered to have increased. Remember that *both* the report of past activity and current activity were asked in 1975. Thus, data on past activities are based on retrospective reports. The assessment of changes in activity levels is drawn from the respondents' evaluations of their current level of activity in 1975, compared with their evaluation of the frequency with which they had engaged in each activity five years previously.

The table shows that the majority of retirees continued to engage in each of the activities shown at the same level as prior to their retirements. Thus, the major pattern is one of continuity, rather than disengagement, and intensification, or substitution, of activities. To be sure, retirees did change their levels of participation in a few activities. Almost half of them increased contacts with relatives—but almost a third decreased such contacts. More than one-quarter of the retirees worked more on hobbies and a fifth did more work around the house. A third of the retirees decreased eating out in restaurants.

Employed respondents also maintained former levels of activities and social involvements. Note, for example, the similar proportions of employed and retired people who increased or decreased getting together with relatives. However, there were a few differences between retirees and workers. Retirees were more likely to say they increased participation in working on hobbies, getting together with neighbors, working around the house and going for walks; they were more likely to report decreasing eating out. Generally retirees who increased activities over the past five years were more likely than the workers to increase their participation in quiet activities at home or in the neighborhood. Some of the activities they decreased—like dining out and cultural activities—involve outlays of money.

If these self-reports can be trusted, the main trend observed is that most retirees do not change their participation in activities and that retirees are not much different in activity from working people their own age. The idea that retirees substitute new activities for the loss of their work roles does

TABLE 3-4. *Five-Year Changes in Activities among One Cohort of Retired and Employed People Aged 64–69 in 1975*

| | Frequency with Which Engaged in Each Activity in 1975 and 5 Years Previously (Self-Reports in 1975) | | | | | | | |
| | Retired between 1971 and 1975 Interviews | | | | Worked at the Time of the 1971 and 1975 Interviews | | | |
Activity	Same %	Less %	More %	Total %	Same %	Less %	More %	Total %
Watches television	84	3	13	2,999[a]	89	4	7	2,403[a]
Gets together with neighbors	60	21	19		70	19	11	
Gets together with relatives	21	30	49		22	32	45	
Reads books, magazines or newspapers	89	6	5		93	4	3	
Works on hobbies	62	10	27		77	10	13	
Works on home maintenance or small repairs around house	63	16	20		78	12	11	
Goes outside	95	4	1		98	1	1	
Goes for walk	66	15	19	2,982[b]	83	9	8	2,398[b]
Participates in sports or exercise	80	12	7		86	11	4	
Goes to club meetings or other organizational activity	70	20	10		79	15	6	
Goes to restaurant	56	34	10		73	16	10	
Goes to church or temple services	80	14	5		87	10	4	
Goes to grocery store	79	9	12		86	7	8	
Goes to concert, play, movie, sports event, or opera	72	21	7		77	17	5	
Does volunteer work	83	8	8		87	8	5	
Takes trip lasting longer than one day	71	18	11		78	15	7	

[a]Actual number reporting on each item varies slightly since small number of individuals did not report on each item.

[b]Interviewers were instructed to skip this and the following items if the respondent was obviously unable to walk. Slight variations on each item with nonreporting.

Based on unpublished data from Retirement History Study, Social Security Administration.

not appear to be true for these retirees. Nor does it appear that they have disengaged—at least at their present ages of 64–69.

Since retirement is defined in Table 3-4 as being out of the labor force, retirees who might be engaged in some kind of paid work are not shown. Some retirees do not sever their connections with the world of work. Between 15–25% of retirees work at paid employment, primarily at part-time jobs. Thus some retirees not only continue in former nonwork activities but also maintain work participation.

Geographical Residence

Retirees, of course, live in all states of the Union but tend to concentrate in certain states. In 1970, almost half of all people 65 and over out of the labor force lived in seven states. Table 3-5 shows the seven states with the largest number of retired persons. Not surprisingly, New York, California, and Pennsylvania had the largest number of retirees 65 and over. They were, after all, the three most populous states in 1970. Actually, New York and Pennsylvania had a somewhat higher proportion of retired persons 65 and over than national averages. But Florida clearly has a disproportionate share of retirees and older people in general. In 1970, 14.5% of Florida's population was 65 and over, compared to 9.8% nationally; 12% of Florida's population was made up of people 65 and over out of the labor force while the national percentage was 7.8%.

TABLE 3-5. *The Seven States with the Largest Number of People Aged 65 and Over out of the Labor Force, 1970*

State	Number out of Labor Force	Total Population
New York	1,509,921	18,236,967
California	1,445,950	19,953,134
Pennsylvania	1,016,452	11,793,909
Florida	842,540	6,789,443
Illinois	833,847	11,113,976
Ohio	787,308	10,652,017
Texas	749,992	11,196,730
U.S. Total	15,759,267	203,210,158

Based on U.S. Bureau of the Census, 1970, 1972a, 1972b.

The concentration of retired people in certain states has consequences for both the retiree and for the state government. States with many retirees are likely to have services and organizations catering to the needs of retirees. In addition, being in areas where there are many retirees means that chances for association with other retired persons and for making acquaintances are quite good. For the state, however, a relatively high proportion of retirees may be a financial burden.

Summary

The more than 18 million retired people in 1979 in the United States share a common experience: they have lost or given up a major social role—the work role. They also tend to be alike in the extent to which they maintain former patterns of nonwork activity. But retirees are not a homogeneous group. Some are comfortable, others are poor; some are in good health, others have serious physical ailments; some are married, others have lost a spouse. They do not all have the same resources for making a good life for themselves without work. If and how these variations among retirees make a difference to their way of life in retirement is one of the themes we pursue in subsequent chapters. In Chapter 4 we explore what appears to be an anomalous situation: according to the data we have reviewed, the way of life of many retirees is constrained in one way or another by losses of economic or social resources. Why is it then that so many older workers choose to retire before age 65?

Review Questions for Chapter 3

1. *What are the factors accounting for the relatively low retirement incomes of women and blacks? What are the prospects for changes in their relative income position?*
2. *Knowing what you now know about the financial situation of retirees, what steps would you take to ensure a comfortable retirement for yourself?*

Early
Retirement

We have already shown that many older people are fully capable of working beyond age 65 and that retirement often entails reduction in income. Further, beliefs that retirement amounts to "laying workers on the shelf" are common. Yet the trend for several decades—up to 1980, at least—has been for increasing numbers of people to retire *before* the age of 65. How can this apparent paradox be explained? Why do older workers decide to retire early? Are older workers being pushed out of their jobs by employers who prefer younger workers and by younger workers who want to take over the slots of the older workers? Or are workers deciding to retire before age 65 because they believe that retirement will prove to be a rewarding period in their lives? Does the trend toward early retirement belie the notion that retirement is a troubled time of life? There are no unequivocal answers to these questions.

To understand workers' motivations for retiring before age 65, we look at what people say about their reasons for retiring early and at the health, social, and economic conditions that seem to encourage early retirement. There may also be subtle and indirect pressures that induce people to retire early but are difficult to document; indeed, the people involved are probably not even aware of such pressures. In general, it appears that many workers retire early not so much because they are actively seeking the retirement role, but because of direct and indirect constraints. At the same time, many of the same workers do have positive attitudes toward retirement.

Before exploring these questions, a word about the number of people involved. One way of measuring the trend in early retirement is to look at trends in the proportion of workers between ages 60 and 64 who have had no work experience for a given year.[1] According to Bixby (1976), in 1974, for example, 16% of men 60–61 had no work experience. At ages 62–64, when they were eligible for **reduced social security benefits** (that is, somewhat less money than they would receive if they retired at age 65 or later), 26% of the men reported no work experience. These percentages are higher than for previous years. As recently as 1970, only 12% of men 60–61, and 21% of those 62–64, were without work experience. The trend for women since 1970 has been somewhat similar (see footnote 1 and Table 4-1).

TABLE 4-1. *Labor Force Participation Rate and Percent with Work Experience during the Year for People 60–64, 1970–1978*

Year	Men		Women	
	Labor Force Rate	Work Experience	Labor Force Rate	Work Experience
1970	75.0	83.2	36.1	47.2
1971	74.1	81.6	36.4	45.6
1972	72.5	80.3	35.4	44.1
1973	69.1	79.6	34.2	44.7
1974	67.9	78.3	33.4	42.8
1975	65.7	73.4	33.3	40.8
1976	63.7	73.4	33.1	40.6
1977	62.9	70.1	32.9	40.6
1978	62.0	70.9	33.1	41.3

Adapted from Bixby, 1976, p. 4, and selected Special Labor Force Reports.

Another way of estimating the trend toward early retirement is to look at the proportion of retired-worker beneficiaries receiving reduced benefits claimed before age 65. In 1978 approximately 70% of the men and women starting to receive retired-worker cash benefits did so before age 65. For the men, this represents a substantial increase even since 1968 when the percentage was 54%. For the women, despite some fluctuations in given years, the proportion with reduced benefits for early retirement has been about the

[1]Figures on work experience during a given year are typically higher than data on labor force status. This occurs because more people will have engaged in some kind of work during the year than are counted in the labor force (working or looking for work) in an average week of that year. Table 4-1 shows figures on both labor force rate and work experience for the years 1970 to 1978 for people aged 60–64.

TABLE 4-2. Number of Newly Awarded Retired-Worker Beneficiaries (OAS-DHI) and Proportion Receiving Reduced Benefits for Early Retirement, 1968–1978

At End of Year[a]	Male Beneficiaries		Female Beneficiaries	
	Total Number (000s)	With Reduction for Early Retirement %	Total Number (000s)	With Reduction for Early Retirement %
1968	677	54	435	71
1969	691	53	449	71
1970	749	53	496	70
1971	752	55	507	71
1973	897	54	650	70
1974	766	63	606	69
1975	873	61	539	89
1976	808	66	569	77
1977	827	70	582	83
1978	781	68	609	73

[a]Data for 1972 are not complete and, therefore, have been omitted from table.

Adapted from *Social Security Bulletin,* September 1979, p. 83.

same over the ten-year period from 1968 to 1978. See Table 4-2, which shows trends since 1968 in the number of people awarded retired-worker benefits and the proportion with reduction for early retirement.

Reasons for Early Retirement

Given such trends, it is tempting to conclude that attitudes toward retirement are becoming increasingly favorable, especially in light of the reduced benefits retirees seem willing to accept. As Table 4-3 shows, in 1978 men with reduced benefits for early retirement received average monthly payments that are $48 lower than men without such reductions; the corresponding figure for women was $50. However, while favorable attitudes may induce some workers to opt for early retirement, other factors may be operating to ease workers out of their jobs before age 65. Given the stereotypes discussed in Chapter 2, it would not be surprising if employers or other workers exerted pressures on older workers to retire. Further, some workers might seize the opportunity to retire before age 65 because of health problems. In other words, while some people undoubtedly retire early because they look forward to retirement, others may do so primarily because of poor health or problems on the job. Several sets of research bear on this issue. Since we will be referring to these studies repeatedly, we want to describe them briefly.

TABLE 4-3. *Average Monthly Retired-Worker Benefits with and without Reduction for Early Retirement*[a]

At End of Year	Without Reduction for Early Retirement		With Reduction for Early Retirement	
	Men	Women	Men	Women
1961	$84	$65	$69	$57
1962	85	66	71	58
1963	87	67	72	58
1964	88	69	73	59
1965	96	75	79	64
1966	97	76	80	65
1967	99	78	82	66
1968	115	92	95	78
1969	118	95	97	79
1970	139	112	115	94
1971	156	126	130	105
1972	192	156	161	130
1973	197	164	164	135
1974	224	186	187	154
1975	247	206	207	169
1976	270	224	226	183
1977	293	242	246	198
1978	320	264	268	214

[a]In current-payment status.

Adapted from Bixby, 1976, p. 6, and *Social Security Bulletin,* September 1979, p. 82.

The studies described below deal with plans for early retirement among mature persons in the labor force and/or with various aspects of retirement among people who have already retired before age 65. Some studies also have data on people who retired at age 65 and later.

The National Longitudinal Surveys (NLS) are based on interviews with a national sample of men who were 45–59 in 1966 and who have been reinterviewed several times over a period of many years. Comparable samples of younger men and women in the labor force and mature working women (age 30–44 in 1966) were also interviewed repeatedly (see, for example, Andrisani & Parnes, 1977; Parnes, Adams, Andrisani, Kohen, & Nestel, 1975; Parnes, Nestel, Chirikos, Daymont, Mott, & Parsons, 1979).

The Retirement History Study (RHS), as noted in Chapter 3, is also a longitudinal study. It has been conducted by the Social Security Administration for a period of ten years. A 50-state sample of men 58–63 and their wives, and of women 58–63 who were not living with a spouse (mostly widows) was interviewed for the first time in 1969 and reinterviewed every other year since then, with the last interviews carried out in 1979. (Studies based on this research are reported, for example, in Bixby, 1976; Bond, 1976; A. Fox, 1976, 1979; Irelan & Bell, 1972; Irelan, Motley, Schwab, Sally R.

Sherman & Murray, 1976; Motley, 1978; Quinn, 1978; Schwab, 1976; Sally R. Sherman, 1976; G. B. Thompson, 1978a, 1978b.)

In 1964, under a contract negotiated by the United Automobile Workers (UAW) with the automobile companies, early retirement provisions of the previously established retirement program were liberalized. The liberalized program made it possible for a qualified worker to retire as early as age 60 with a maximum $400 monthly pension or, at ages 55–60, with a lower pension. In either case, the company pension was subject to reduction at age 65. The Automobile Workers Study (AWS) is based on a 1967 survey of a random sample from ages 59–63 and a resurvey of these workers in late 1969 and early 1970. (The results are reported in Barfield & Morgan, 1970.)

A National Sample Survey (NSS), conducted by the Survey Research Center of the University of Michigan, was undertaken to complement the Automobile Workers Study. It is based on a representative sample of people living in private households in the mainland United States. The data reported here focus on family heads aged 35–59. Unlike the other studies we have just mentioned, it is a cross-section survey, giving a snapshot of the sample at one point in time. (This study is also reported in Barfield & Morgan, 1970.)

All in all, these studies provide us with a wealth of data, much of which was not available when theoretical approaches to retirement were first being formulated.

Planning Early Retirement

What can be learned from people's expressed plans to retire early? After all, people planning to retire early may not carry out their plans. If retirement is 20 years in the future and a person's job is not particularly exciting, the individual may idealize retirement. Or there may be obstacles to early retirement, regardless of personal plans. For example, some people may have children still to put through school. Nonetheless, we feel that self-reported plans for retirement are important. First, as it turns out, there appears to be a correlation between planning to retire early and actually doing so. At least among the auto workers, most people who planned to retire early did carry out their plans (Barfield & Morgan, 1970). Second, planning early retirement is not distributed randomly in the population of mature workers. By identifying the kinds of people most likely to plan early retirement, we uncover clues about motivations for retiring early.

The most important single factor related to planning early retirement is *economic*. Consider the following:

- Planning early retirement was most likely among those who thought they could look forward to liberal retirement benefits (Andrisani & Parnes, 1977).
- Among household heads 35–59, the amount of pension and annuity income

expected was positively related to planning early retirement (Barfield & Morgan, 1970).

- Among auto workers, almost one-third of the eligible workers had already retired at the time of the first interviews in 1967 and another one-third were planning to retire before age 65. The likelihood of having an adequate retirement income, given the financial responsibilities of the workers, was associated with having retired early or planning to retire early (Barfield & Morgan, 1970).

Thus it appears that the prospect of retirement is pleasing if the individual feels he or she can maintain an adequate standard of living. However, other factors associated both with planning early retirement and with having actually retired before age 65 suggest that it is not the appeal of retirement as much as personal and job-related factors that are pushing many older workers off the job.

Theories about the importance of work and the impact of the work ethic tend to underplay the unattractive aspects of many jobs. Not all people are committed to work or to their particular jobs. As it turns out, studies suggest that those who are dissatisfied with their jobs, who have relatively unfavorable attitudes toward work in general, are most likely to plan to retire early (Andrisani & Parnes, 1977; Barfield & Morgan, 1970). Further, there are often perceived pressures that induce the worker to plan to retire before age 65. For example, those who thought younger workers wanted older ones to retire to make jobs available were somewhat more likely to plan to retire before 65 than their counterparts (Barfield & Morgan, 1970). Auto workers who had experienced recent changes in the nature of their jobs, as through automation, and auto workers who found their workplace unpleasant were somewhat more likely to plan to retire early than other auto workers their age (Barfield & Morgan, 1970).

Finally, perceiving that one's health is poor (or professing such perceptions) is related both to planning early retirement and, even more strongly, to having retired early.

Retiring Early

In general, the same factors that are mentioned as reasons for planning early retirement influence the actual retirement decision.

Health. One of the most consistent findings about people who have retired before 65 is that a high proportion of them cite poor health as the major reason for their decision to retire early. But is it actually poor health? We can imagine that early retirees (or those who plan to retire early) cite health as a reason for their decisions because it seems to be a legitimate reason for not working. As Parsons' (1951) analysis of the sick role suggests, being sick is not merely a physical condition; it constitutes a social role with a set of expectations for how to behave. When people are sick, expectations are generally relaxed; the sick are permitted behaviors not approved for healthy people. For example, the sick are relieved of responsibilities and can be dependent. If the work ethic is pervasive, then retired people may feel that poor health is the only justifiable reason for voluntarily giving up work.

The available evidence indicates that many early retirees *are* in poor health. For one thing, as noted previously, older people's perceptions of their health are generally in accord with physicians' ratings, sometimes even more positive than the physicians' evaluations (Riley & Foner, 1968). In addition, health statistics on older people in general show increasing mortality and morbidity rates with aging (Riley & Foner, 1968). Finally, there is specific evidence of poor health among early retirees. For example, men 58–63 who had retired early were more likely than those still in the labor force to have been hospitalized the previous year and to have visited a physician (Schwab, 1976). The National Longitudinal Survey found that men aged 45–59 who reported health problems that limited the kind or amount of work they could do in 1966 were more likely than the "healthy" to have died five years later, by 1971 (Andrisani, 1977).

Even assuming that people who report they are in poor health are suffering from some ailment, it is possible that some of their physiological or psychological symptoms stem from pressures on the job. That is, there may be a two-way relationship between health and the job. We know that many illnesses can be activated by stress or other psychological problems. Thus, while poor health may induce some to retire from their work before age 65, deteriorating conditions of work (or what are perceived as deteriorating conditions) can trigger or exacerbate illness.

Further, poor health does not inevitably lead to early retirement. Some individuals have had debilitating strokes, have lost limbs, or have had serious respiratory problems that make work impossible; others have infirmities that may not affect their work or that make daily work uncomfortable, but not impossible. The Retirement History Study provides data that bear on this point. In 1969 about one-third of the women and men 58–63 who were interviewed reported some type of health-related limitation and these were more likely to be out of the labor force than those who reported no such limitation. Nevertheless, about 60% of the men and one-third of the women with self-reported work limitations were still in the labor force. To understand what induces some people with work limitations to leave the labor force and what induces others similarly limited to keep working, we must consider other factors influencing the early retirement decision (Irelan et al., 1976).

Money and the Job. Recall the importance of income and job pressures as factors in *plans* for early retirement. Estimates of retirement income and job characteristics are also influential in the decision to retire early among people in poor health as well as those in good health. For example, quite apart from health or age, second-pension coverage or even the expectation of adequate retirement income is related to early withdrawal from the labor force (Barfield & Morgan, 1970; Bixby, 1976). In addition, there is a slight association between having a job with undesirable attributes—bad working conditions such as extreme temperatures, noise, odors, hazards, toxic conditions, dust, or poor ventilation; physical or mental strains on the job; or having little or no opportunity to exercise independent action or judgment on the job—and early withdrawal from the labor force (Quinn, 1978). In this regard, several other findings are of interest. For example, professionals and managers, presumably those with interesting jobs and a good deal of autonomy, are less likely to retire early than blue-collar workers and workers in clerical positions, those whose jobs are probably less interesting (Bixby, 1976). People with high commitment to their jobs and high job satisfaction are less likely to have retired early than those with less job commitment and lower job satisfaction (Bixby, 1976). Thus it appears that the availability of an adequate retirement income on the one hand and unattractive job conditions on the other are both related to early retirement.

Clearly, then, factors other than health motivate workers to leave their jobs before age 65. However, cross-section data from the Retirement History Study indicate that males who reported poor health were more likely than those who reported good health either to take advantage of financial inducements to retire early or to withdraw from a job with unpleasant working conditions (Quinn, 1978). Thus, it appears that for those in poor health, it is often a combination of factors and not poor health alone that triggers the decision to retire early.

The Push-Pull Factors in Early Retirement

Whatever the particular factors involved, we can only conclude that much early retirement is not voluntary. For many people, early retirement provides an escape from a work situation that is uncomfortable—either because of poor health, the nature of the job, pressures from other workers, or some combination. Other external factors serve to propel older workers out of the labor force. For example, when labor market conditions are poor, some unemployed older workers who cannot find other work decide to take advantage of social security benefits and do retire early (Sheppard, 1977). Given any of these factors that heighten the propensity of workers to withdraw from the labor force before age 65—poor health, unpleasant job situation, an unfavorable labor market—the availability of an adequate income makes it possible for them to actually retire early.

Not all retirees are "involuntary" retirees. A considerable number are attracted by the opportunity to enjoy leisure activities. For example, a 58-year-old steel worker planning to retire at age 58 with a $700-a-month pension remarked, "I've been working since I was 10 years old. I want to get the heck out and enjoy some of my life while I can" ("When Retirement Doesn't Happen," 1978). Of course, the pull of a life of leisure is often not sufficient to prompt such workers to retire early. They too must feel that their retirement income will be adequate when they decide to retire before age 65.

Given the importance of an adequate retirement income to all early retirees, the overall economic context of the preretirement years is a powerful influence on the retirement decision. Many of the subjects in these studies spent a good part of their adult lives in prosperity just after World War II and established themselves during a relatively long period of economic growth. They may have bought a home before the recent skyrocketing of house prices and came along late enough to accumulate private pension benefits (Barfield & Morgan, 1978a). The inflation and spotty employment picture of the 1970s may well discourage new cohorts on the threshold of retirement in the 1980s from withdrawing from the labor force before they are 65. The value of people's savings has been reduced. For some, there has been the threat or even the reality of unemployment, which is likely to reduce the person's confidence that enough can be saved for an early retirement. In addition, questions have been raised about the solvency and equity of some private pension plans. All such trends raise doubts about having sufficient retirement income and are likely to make future cohorts uncertain about financial security in their retirement years (Barfield & Morgan, 1978a). More generally, the life experiences of each cohort of potential retirees influence the retirement decisions of members of these different cohorts. If economic conditions deteriorate, future cohorts—however favorable their attitudes to retirement may be—may reverse present trends in early retirement.

We started out by asking whether the trend toward early retirement heralds new, favorable attitudes toward retirement. At first the evidence seems ambiguous: only some retirees seem drawn to retirement by the opportunity to enjoy their remaining years in leisure pursuits, free of work responsibilities; others are pushed out of their jobs by direct or indirect pressures. It would be misleading, however, to conclude that widespread "involuntary" early retirement implies negative attitudes toward retirement. Many of those pushed out of their jobs seem as likely as the "voluntary" retirees to look favorably on retirement. Indeed, most early retirees hold positive preretirement attitudes (Bixby, 1976). Such positive attitudes are understandable in light of the evidence we have reviewed. If early retirement gives the "voluntary" retirees the chance to engage in activities they had little time for when they were working, it also gives the "involuntary" early retirees a viable alternative to distressful jobs.

Thus, whether early retirees left their jobs because they were pushed out or because they were pulled by the attractions of retired life under the social and economic conditions that prevailed in the 1960s and most of the 1970s, early retirement offered retirees benefits. It is noteworthy that even with high inflation there was a continued, if slight, decline in labor-force participation rates of men aged 55–64, as of the first five months of 1979

(Parnes, 1979). But there are no clear signs to indicate whether social and economic conditions in the next decades will remain auspicious for early retirees or whether the trend toward early retirement will continue in the 1980s.

Review Questions
for Chapter 4

1. *Identify several reasons for early retirement based on material presented in this chapter. What kinds of alternatives to early retirement might be developed to satisfy the needs that now lead to early retirement?*
2. *What problems does the researcher face in determining the importance of poor health as a factor motivating workers to retire early? How might the researcher solve some of these problems?*
3. *Discuss how cohort experiences can influence the trend toward early retirement.*
4. *What are the implications of the trend toward early retirement for the meaning of work in contemporary American society?*

5

Fitting into the Retirement Role

Whether people retire "early," "on time," or "late," they must build their lives around retirement instead of work. In this chapter we focus on how people fit into the retirement role. Just as there are stereotypes about older workers, there are stereotypes about retirement; many people believe that retirement amounts to "putting the elderly on the shelf." The transition to retirement is considered especially stressful. The following words from Jaffe (1972) state the situation forcefully:

> Our society has stressed the work ethic with its accompanying assumption that leisure is undesirable. That many men have trouble in overcoming this ethic and accepting leisure as a moral way of life is clearly evident from the efforts being made to "prepare men for retirement." Such preparation means undoing a lifetime of habits, undoing the work ethic under which the man grew up and spent his working lifetime. That many men never overcome their original upbringing is evidenced by the retiree's complaints of being socially useless, "being put out to grass," having no purpose in life [p. 76].

There are others who also speak of retirement as a crisis (Glick, 1977; Miller, 1965) or as traumatic (Withers, 1974). For some retirement is seen as a burden, even an affliction.

These views about retirement are based on several assumptions—for one, that work contributes to our sense of well-being. A good deal of evidence indicates that this assumption is correct: at least among men in their prime years, work *is* significant for psychological and physiological well-being. Studies of unemployed workers have found many adverse reactions to long periods without work—loss of self-esteem, deterioration in interpersonal relations, and withdrawal from social interaction (Liem & Liem, 1978; Riley, Foner, Hess, & Toby, 1969). For example, among the long-term unemployed during the Great Depression of the 1930s, few individuals found activities that served even partially as a substitute for lost employment. Some unemployed evidenced deep despair—depression, hopelessness, or a sense of futility. Perhaps the most common response was withdrawal and doing nothing most of the day (Riley et al., 1969; Jahoda, Lazarsfeld, & Zeisel, 1933). The belief that loss of work may be harmful undoubtedly lies behind the injunction to the retired to "keep busy." But there's the rub: there are no clear prescriptions for what to keep busy at.

Another assumption behind the dismal judgments of retirement is based on the potentially negative consequences of discontinuities in the transition from work to retirement: the contrast between the role of worker and of retiree, as well as the contradiction between the values epitomized by work and those symbolized by leisure. Elements that might reduce these discontinuities and help create smooth role transitions are generally absent in the transition to retirement: For example, people making other role transitions—to worker, spouse, student—can model their behavior not only after the numerous other people in such roles in their immediate environment, but also after images provided by the mass media. They can rehearse in advance some aspects of their prospective roles. But consider the situation of prospective retirees. Although role models are available, these role models are not as public and visible as role models for people approaching worker, spousal, and student roles. And while a few firms offer extra months vacation or shorter work days in the final work years, for most workers there is little opportunity to rehearse the retirement role in advance.

The things that are missing—clear role definitions, public role models, and chances to rehearse the role—make the transition to retirement unique and can create many difficulties. These difficulties are compounded by the fact that the transition to retirement often involves reductions in income, social esteem, and power. It is no wonder so many commentators hold bleak views of retirement.

If we base our predictions about reactions to retired life on theory and research about other **life-course transitions**, then we should expect people to be reluctant to retire and, once retired, to be dissatisfied with life in retirement. In fact, as we have shown, men are increasingly likely to retire early—before age 65. And, as we discuss below, most retirees say they *like* retired life. These trends seem to contradict theories about life-course transitions and negative views of retirement. In the following pages we will explore these seeming contradictions; we will consider what retired people themselves say about retirement and why they react the way they do; whether there are factors that counterbalance the negative features of the transition to retirement; and the circumstances that help make the transition to retirement either smooth or difficult.

We have already described in Chapter 3 some important aspects of the life styles of retirees—many have to watch their budgets, few of them work, but there is considerable continuity in social relations and activities. Here we focus on retirees' subjective reactions. How do they experience life in retirement? Is it rewarding, as some of them expected? Or is it a period of discontent?

Satisfaction with Retirement

When retired people are asked about how they like retirement, most express a relatively high degree of satisfaction with retired life. For instance, one national longitudinal survey based on interviews with the same people before and after retirement found very positive attitudes toward retirement, as far back as the mid-1950s. Several years after their retirement, the vast majority said "Retirement is mostly good for a person." Only 4–5% said that retirement had turned out worse than they expected (Streib & Schneider, 1971).

Still other examples come from numerous national cross-section surveys, where retirees were questioned at one point in time. From the mid-1960s to the late 1970s, the pattern of response of retirees was remarkably consistent.[1]

- In 1965, 61% of retired persons said that retirement had fulfilled their expectations (Riley & Foner, 1968).
- In 1968, 65% of retired men 65 and over had medium or high morale, as measured by such items as age-image, feelings of usefulness, happiness now as compared to younger years, and feeling that things are the same as or better than the person thought they would be (G. B. Thompson, 1973).
- In 1968, another nationwide study found that three-quarters of the retired people interviewed said they found retirement enjoyable (Barfield & Morgan, 1970).
- In 1971, 63% of the retirees said they were glad they had retired when they did (Campbell, Converse, & Rodgers, 1976).
- In 1973, 55% of those who had retired from seven large corporations—people of relatively high education and occupational status—said "These are the best years of my life." And 83% expected interesting and pleasant things to happen to them in the future (Kimmel, Price, & Walker, 1978).

[1]Although retired women were included in many of the surveys, most of the reports do not separate the responses of men and women. Studies that do provide data for both male and female retirees are not consistent; they do not suggest, as some had hypothesized, that women are more satisfied with retirement than men (Jaslow, 1976; Streib & Schneider, 1971).

- In 1974, 65% of retired or unemployed people 65 and over said they would *not* like to return to work (Harris, 1975).
- In 1976, 56% of retired respondents said they felt good or very good about their lives since retirement (Barfield & Morgan, 1978b).
- In 1978, 65% of retired employees said the quality of retired life is the same or better than life when they were working; 41% said it was somewhat or much better (Harris, 1979).

The evidence is impressive. But do the retirees really mean it? Studies have found that of all age strata, older people are most likely to express satisfaction with life in general or with particular domains of their lives, such as their jobs, homes, and family. One study suggests, however (Campbell et al., 1976), that there is a distinction between feeling satisfied and feeling happy. High levels of satisfaction among the old were combined with relatively low levels of happiness—findings that suggest that people lower their expectations as they grow older. That is, older people say they are satisfied with their lives because they don't expect a great deal in later years. For example, ask an older person "How are you doing?" or "How do you feel?" and the response is likely to be "Not so bad for an old man (or lady)." That there may be latent problems among the old is reflected in the low levels of happiness they report (Riley & Waring, 1976).

Such doubts about retirees' real satisfaction with retirement, however, are counterbalanced by indirect evidence that retirees are *not* unhappy with retired life per se. For one thing, in 1974, relatively few retirees (31%) indicated that they would like to return to work (Harris, 1975). Undoubtedly many retirees felt they could not return to work or find the kinds of jobs they could manage, given health problems and work limitations. But even among retirees with no work limitations, some research found few would be available to return to work (Motley, 1978).

By 1978, retirees' responses were somewhat different, and we believe that the apparent increase in the proportion of retirees saying they prefer to work was primarily a reflection of concerns about inflationary trends. In 1978 a national survey asked two questions relevant to this issue. First, retirees (a small proportion of whom were working part-time or full-time) were asked if they preferred to work now (if working) or *would* prefer to work now (if not working). Forty-six percent said they preferred to work or would prefer to work. Among those receiving pension benefits the proportion was 40% compared to 52% for those not receiving pension benefits. Second, retirees were asked to look back and, assuming that they would have adequate retirement income, indicate whether they would have preferred to retire at the normal retirement age for their type of employment, retire early, continue to work full-time, or work part-time. Fifty-three percent said they would have preferred to continue to work full- or part-time. Again, among those receiving pension benefits, the proportion was lower: 47% compared to 56% for those not receiving pension benefits (Harris, 1979). Two aspects of these data suggest that economic incentives—more than dissatisfaction with retired life—

were the key factors in wanting to work after retirement: first, the fact that the increase from the early 1970s to 1978 in the proportion of retirees preferring to work parallels the increase in inflation in the society and, second, the fact that those without pension benefits, as compared to those with pension benefits, were more likely to say they wanted to work and less likely to say in retrospect that they would have preferred to retire early or at the normal age of retirement.

Further, if retirement leads to latent frustration and discontent, we might expect these strains to be expressed in illness. The evidence is not all in, and many subtle pressures are suspected. So far, however, the weight of research does not support this expectation. While rates of illness do increase with age, retirement in itself does not appear to have a negative effect on health (Atchley, 1976; Friedmann & Orbach, 1974). If anything, most retirees feel that their health stayed the same or improved after retirement (Barfield & Morgan, 1970; Streib & Schneider, 1971).

To sum up, according to studies from the mid-1950s to the late 1970s, the majority of retired people express a good deal of satisfaction with retirement. Although retirees' expression of satisfaction may be somewhat exaggerated, the majority do not want to return to work even in the inflationary late 1970s and retirement, in itself, does not seem to lead to widespread deterioration in health. This is not to say that retired life is all smooth sailing. Many retirees miss things associated with work—their work mates, the feeling of being useful, the money they used to make, and the work itself (Harris, 1975). The consistent findings that most retirees feel satisfied with retirement suggest that most retired workers have learned to live with such losses and find compensations in not working. There is little support in the research for the stereotypical view of retirement as a major life crisis for most people and a conspiracy against the aged.

Doing Something Right—The Making of a Good Retirement

To understand why most retirees seem to be content with retired life, let's look again at some of the factors thought to be associated with retirement difficulties—discontinuities in the transition to retirement, the loss of work roles that contribute to a sense of purpose in life, and reduction in power, prestige, and income. Are there conditions that serve to offset these difficulties? Let's consider several of them: preparation for retirement, activities that substitute for work, and personal resources. Our focus is on characteristics and activities of the individual—what people *did* about retirement before they retired, what they *do* in retirement, and what resources they *have* to help make a go of retired life. In the following chapter we discuss family, community, and social factors that may also affect responses to retirement.

Easing the Transition to Retirement

If a major difficulty in fitting into the retirement role is the abruptness of changes in the person's life at the point of transition from work to nonwork, then any processes that serve to minimize these sharp changes should foster positive reactions to retirement. Advance preparation—either conscious or unconscious—is one such process. In addition, simply having some experience in the role may offset initial problems. The evidence on these matters is meager, but studies do suggest that at least some informal processes of anticipatory socialization are associated with satisfaction with retirement.

Sociologists use the term *anticipatory socialization* to refer to the process of learning attitudes and behaviors associated with a role before the individual is actually in the role. Anticipatory socialization is often casual and unwitting; but conscious or not, the process is thought to ease the transition from one role to another and thus reduce the trauma associated with a drastic role change. Consider familiar examples of anticipatory socialization for other life transitions: dating and going steady serve as partial preparation for marital roles; mock elections in high school give adolescents a taste of what it is like to participate in citizen duties; children away at college pave the way for the "empty nest." Not all anticipatory socialization involves actual role rehearsal, as in the instances cited above. The process may merely entail adopting the attitudes and values that are appropriate for future roles. For example, working-class people hoping to rise in the world often adopt middle-class values and behaviors before they have actually moved into the higher class (Merton, 1957).

Anticipatory socialization for retirement, however, seems more problematic than these examples. Without clear prescriptions about what to do in retirement, rehearsing the role is difficult. Nevertheless, there are some informal and formal practices that can orient people to retirement roles.

First, there is some conscious planning for retirement, although few people do a great deal of it (Kasschau, 1974; Riley & Foner, 1968). Some people simply plan the age at which they will retire. Some may estimate their benefits, while others make more specific financial arrangements. Still others plan to move, go to school, work part-time, or undertake leisure activities.

Second, there are formal counseling programs sponsored by some companies or unions. Here retirees may receive information about finances and social security regulations, even if only to be able to compute their benefits. They may also have the opportunity to discuss health, leisure, and other related issues. However, personal counseling programs are quite limited. For example, among 800 large United States companies (the majority had 1000 or more employees), 88% did offer some preretirement assistance to employees. But most companies offer only financial information—about pensions, social security benefits, or insurance. Some companies also offer information about Medicare and supplemental medical benefits. Only 13% of the companies provide personal counseling on a variety of matters like financial planning, housing arrangements, legal matters, use of leisure time, and the like (O'Meara, 1977).

Third, although most retirees do relatively little specific planning for retirement, many individuals experience unwitting processes of anticipatory socialization for retirement. That is, some prospective retirees adopt favorable attitudes toward retirement before they are retired; they orient themselves and look forward to it. This process may be more widespread than formal preparation.

Do any of these formal or informal processes have an effect on satisfaction with retirement? To some extent; probably most important are preretirement attitudes. One longitudinal study of retirees in the 1950s found that those who had looked favorably upon retirement in advance and who had a good idea of what retirement would be like were more likely than others not only to accept the loss of the work role but also to take less than three months to get used to not working and to have no difficulty keeping busy (W. E. Thompson, 1958; see also Kimmel et al., 1978). Merely planning when to retire and carrying out these plans is a help, whereas retiring unexpectedly seems to interfere with the enjoyment of retirement (Barfield & Morgan, 1970). Some studies suggest that more formal planning and participation in counseling programs may also be associated with positive attitudes after retirement (Friedmann & Orbach, 1974). However, we cannot tell from these studies whether a self-selection process is operating. That is, it may be that those most favorably disposed to retirement are the ones most likely to plan ahead and to participate in formal programs.

Some form of advance preparation for retirement is likely to be a help in later adjustment to retirement. But there can also be pitfalls in such processes of anticipatory socialization. Consider another life-course transition, the transition to motherhood. Anticipatory socialization based on idealized views of motherhood's joy and fulfillment with little thought of the difficulties and responsibilities can hinder rather than help adjustment to the maternal role and may result in disillusion or feelings of incompetence (Riley & Waring, 1976). Similarly, plans for retirement based on unrealistic views can create frustrations and disappointments later on. Alternatively, as we have seen, having an idea of what retirement will be like is linked with positive reactions to retirement. But, in these everchanging times, it may be difficult for prospective retirees to have an accurate perception of what the future role will be like. For example, company programs can help future retirees estimate their retirement income accurately and can discuss the retiree's rights. But these programs will not be able to tell retirees what their dollars will buy if economic conditions remain unstable, what their neighborhoods will be like in the future, or what prevailing attitudes about retirement will be in coming years. Thus, it makes sense that much role learning takes place only *after* the individual has retired. And, for those who have already retired, this learning apparently takes relatively little time; most retirees say they got used to retirement in less than a year (Atchley, 1976; Streib & Schneider, 1971).

In sum, retirees do relatively little conscious planning ahead for retirement, but this does not really seem to retard adaptation to the retirement role. Actually, as the material on early retirement suggests, many retirees *are* being socialized for retirement in one way—they are being socialized to give up the work role. Over the life course, socialization for new roles involves two processes: learning to leave old roles and learning the appropriate behaviors and attitudes of the new roles. In the case of retirement, as the worker grows older, commitments to the work role are loosened as the individual finds the rewarding aspects of work reduced or taken away. In such a manner, the older worker is being prepared for role *exit* (Riley et al., 1969). At the same time, an informal, but quite effective, form of anticipatory socialization for *entry* into the new role does occur as individuals adopt favorable attitudes to retirement in their preretirement years. Such attitudes are, at least in part, related to the person's life situation—for example, her or his financial outlook in retirement (Glamser, 1976; Riley & Foner, 1968; Sheppard, 1976). But the spread of favorable attitudes to retirement also owes much to the climate of opinion in the whole society, something we will discuss more fully in the next chapter.

Keeping Busy

It is commonly believed that if retired workers are to have a good retirement, they must find activities that will substitute for the loss of work—either by engaging in new roles or by increasing the time spent in familiar roles. In this view, work is seen as serving more than economic functions. While the meaning of work may vary among different occupational groups, an implicit assumption behind advice to remain active is that work serves to integrate the individual into the society and gives form to the daily routine. Thus, according to this line of thinking, a sense of well-being can be maintained in retirement only if the individual remains "connected" to society and finds activities to fill the free time. (For fuller discussion of activity theories of aging, see Kuypers & Bengtson, 1973; Lemon et al., 1972; Shanas, 1972).

Most retirees do keep at least moderately busy. They do things around the house; they read, garden, play golf; some participate in clubs; they see their friends and relatives (Bengtson, 1969; Harris, 1975). And there appears to be an association between activity and a sense of well-being among retired people—as among older people in general (Barfield & Morgan, 1970; Campbell et al., 1976; Larson, 1978; Sheldon, McEwan, & Ryser, 1975).

The positive relationship between activity and satisfaction with retirement, however, remains ambiguous. For one thing, it is not always clear how retirees' health or **socioeconomic status** is involved in the relationship between activities and sense of well-being. Yet retirees in poor health or of low socioeconomic status are more likely to be the ones with low levels of activity, so it may be poor health or low socioeconomic status that is the major factor in these people's relative dissatisfaction with retirement. Indeed, among samples of people 65 and over in general, once health and socioeconomic status are controlled in the analysis, the association between life satisfaction and at least one kind of activity—participation in voluntary associations—becomes nonsignificant (Bull & Aucoin, 1975; Cutler, 1973).[2]

Second, although retirees do find activities that structure their days and serve to maintain their links with society, they do so in myriad ways not captured by answers to simple survey questions. These answers cannot register the quality of activity and social interaction in which retirees engage. Even the few longitudinal studies that deal with this issue do not convey the full meaning of increasing or decreasing levels of activity. For example, a retired person can slow down and yet remain active and engaged. Maybe surveys don't reflect fully the desire of a good number of retirees to ease off. As one retiree told Atchley (1976, p. 98), "It's nice not to have to keep up the pace anymore." That there are a substantial number of other retirees who welcome such a decrease in activities is suggested by the 1978 Harris survey. Among retirees who had said that retired life is better than working life, 49% also said it was because they could do anything they pleased, had no schedule to meet and could get away from routine. Another 37% said it was because they could take it easier, and didn't have to push or had no worries (Atchley, 1976; Harris, 1979; Riley & Foner, 1968; Streib & Schneider, 1971).

Personal Resources: Health and Socioeconomic Status

Health and wealth, folksayings have it, are two of the most important ingredients of the good life. Research on older people's reactions to retired life lend support to the popular wisdom. Perceiving one's health as good and

---

[2]A few other studies, in effect, control for socioeconomic status by focusing on homogeneous populations, but their results are inconsistent and difficult to interpret. For example, among former blue-collar auto workers, those who increased, or at least maintained, a variety of activities—such as home-based painting and redecorating or even taking an interest in newsworthy events—were more likely than those who did not engage in such retirement activities to show satisfaction with retirement (Barfield & Morgan, 1970). Alternatively, among a sample of middle-class and upper-middle-class people soon to move to a retirement community, there was no relationship between life satisfaction and frequency of involvement with solitary activities, with participation in formal organizations, or even with frequency of informal interaction with relatives and neighbors. The only statistically significant relationship was that between frequency of informal interaction with friends and life satisfaction (Lemon, Bengtson, & Peterson, 1972). The different outcomes of these two studies may represent different measures used, class differences, the special nature of each of these populations (relatively advantaged auto workers and relatively well-off people moving to a retirement community), or methods of analysis. In any event the confusing results merely underscore the ambiguity of the relationship between life satisfaction and activity.

---

having relatively high socioeconomic status are both associated with positive feelings about retirement. While health and socioeconomic status are themselves associated—people of higher status tend to be in better health than those in lower status—each of these factors is independently related to satisfaction with retirement.[3]

Consider health: the English novelist Laurence Sterne wrote: "Oh Blessed health. He that has this has little more to wish for." Such a sentiment is echoed by many retirees. They often express their joy at merely being alive and able to carry on their daily lives with so few restrictions. Despite the pervasiveness of chronic conditions like high blood pressure or arthritis in the older population, most retired people are not limited in their major activities and tend to evaluate their health positively. Those who do have serious health concerns and who are restricted are more likely than their more fortunate peers to express dissatisfaction with their lives. Responses of auto workers to the question, "Generally speaking, how do you feel about your life since retirement?" illustrate the mood of retirees in poor health (Barfield & Morgan, 1970, p. 152):

> Disgusted. I can't do anything because of my lungs. Have to watch every step I make.
>
> I never feel good since I had this stroke.
>
> To tell you the truth it's been kind of rotten—have to spend so much time in bed.

Barfield and Morgan conclude that the major source of dissatisfaction among retired auto workers was health problems.

As for socioeconomic position, we have already suggested that this is a key factor in the individual's sense of well-being. Sociological research has consistently demonstrated that the person's financial position, educational level, and occupational prestige influence her or his ways of thinking and acting. Socioeconomic status is associated with diverse behaviors and attitudes: for example, morbidity and mortality, consumption patterns, leisure behavior, voting, self-esteem, satisfaction with life or work or marriage. Those with high social benefits are generally also high on scales of nonwork activity, happiness, health, and evaluation of self (Foner, 1979). It is not surprising, then, that the retiree's socioeconomic standing is an important influence on the reaction to retirement.

Retirement income, in particular, is a key resource. As we have shown in Chapter 3, on the average, retirees suffer almost a 50% reduction in income when they retire. But there is wide variation both in preretirement income and in the ratio of current to preretirement income. There are some

[3]There are likely to be complex relationships among these variables. For example, while low socioeconomic status may be a factor in poor health, poor health may lead to low socioeconomic status; similarly, good health may influence satisfaction with retirement, but satisfaction with retirement may also contribute to good health.

retired people who have more than 100% of their preretirement income, while others have much less than half.

According to the Retirement History Study, it is nonmarried women who are particularly disadvantaged. Many of them retired early, and few have private or government pensions to supplement their social security benefits (A. Fox, 1976). Thus, for some retirees reduction in income means that they cannot maintain their previous standard of living or even maintain a *minimum* standard of living. In this regard, a 1978 survey found that 42% of retired people said they had less than an adequate standard of living; and, not unexpectedly, financial concerns were the chief complaints of retirees who said retired life was worse than working life (Harris, 1979). Other retirees feel fewer constraints on their lifestyle. And, as we would expect, retirees with the highest incomes and those who feel financially secure are the ones most likely to be satisfied with retirement (Barfield & Morgan, 1970, 1978b; Chatfield, 1977; Friedmann & Orbach, 1974; Heidbreder, 1972; Jaslow, 1976; G. B. Thompson, 1973). It is not only that these better-off retirees have fewer financial worries and can more easily maintain their standard of living, but also that having money permits them to engage in pleasurable and meaningful activities. Many activities require substantial outlays—travel, sports, and the like. Even participating in organizations often entails a wardrobe and transportation expenses. In short, money helps.

Studies have also found that educational level is associated with satisfaction with retirement (Barfield & Morgan, 1970; Campbell et al., 1976; Heidbreder, 1972). In part, education contributes to satisfaction with retirement because education is positively associated with income: the higher the educational attainment, the higher the individual's income, on the average. The more highly educated retirees also seem to have a great variety of interests.

In short, being healthy, wealthy, and wise seem to be key elements in a good retirement.

Conclusion

The evidence we have reviewed in this chapter does not support the bleak predictions about retired life. The trend to early retirement indicates that many older workers themselves think that retired life offers advantages. And once retired, a majority of retirees appear to find retired life agreeable. They are especially likely to enjoy retirement if they are in good health and have an adequate income. Having financial resources is, in turn, associated with other factors that are also related to a "good" retirement such as favorable preretirement attitudes and participation in cultural, recreational, and organizational activities.

One reason for the myth of the unhappy retiree is an overemphasis on the intrinsic satisfactions of work—perhaps a reflection of the middle-class bias of commentators and professionals. Not all workers are satisfied with their jobs, the proportion expressing high satisfaction with their work decreasing as occupational level declines. Among dissatisfied workers especially, jobs do not provide many intrinsic satisfactions like interesting work and responsibility (Andrisani, Appelbaum, Koppel, & Miljus, 1977). Workers who are not satisfied with their jobs often welcome the chance to retire.

Theories about what contributes to a satisfactory retirement also frequently ignore societal influences. Both activity and anticipatory-socialization theories emphasize what the individual does. Yet this depends a great deal on resources provided by the larger society. And, as we show in the next chapter, social and economic programs for retirees have expanded in recent decades.

Favorable preretirement attitudes also play an important part in subsequent responses to retirement; these attitudes, in turn, are influenced by the prevailing attitudes in the whole society. Further, the climate of opinion in society is not static. Recent cohorts of retirees have begun retirement in quite a different—and more favorable—atmosphere than earlier cohorts for whom retirement may have indeed been a crisis. Retirement, unlike unemployment among younger workers, is now considered a *right;* as you will see, it is increasingly defined as a reward for a lifetime of work.

In short, a full understanding of the impact of retirement on the individual requires consideration of social resources made available to retirees and of changing social attitudes.

We do not want to overemphasize satisfaction with retirement among retirees. As we have shown, retirement does not turn out to be gratifying for a good number of people. Of the many individual characteristics that undoubtedly account for dissatisfaction with retirement, poor health and low income are key. For too many retirees there is, then, a contradiction between social definitions of the retirement role as a reward for a lifetime of work and the actual benefits they receive. It is socially imposed **downward mobility** that is one of the most pressing problems. We say "socially imposed" because economic and other resources available to the individual are influenced by factors beyond the individual, at least at this stage of life. For example, income levels are affected by the world situation, the state of the economy, social security and other legislation, and the soundness of private pensions. Poor health, which constitutes another major problem for the retiree, is also something over which he or she has little control in the later years.

Thus, although we began by asking what it is that the individual does (or did) to lay the groundwork for an enjoyable retirement, we conclude that it is just as important what society does. Providing a favorable climate of opinion helps to define retirement as rewarding rather than oppressive, which in turn encourages anticipatory socialization for retirement. And providing adequate social and economic resources helps to ensure that retirees will have the means to live comfortably and to pursue their interests. In the next chapter we consider this theme more fully, as well as the impact of the retiree's social networks.

1. What questions would you include in a survey of older people to determine whether they were truly satisfied with their lives?
2. Are studies of unemployment among adults under 65 relevant to understanding loss of work as a result of retirement?
3. Do you agree that planning ahead for retirement is important for having a good life in retirement?
4. Discuss the interplay between socioeconomic status, health, activity, and satisfaction with retirement.

6

Family, Community, and Societal Context

No matter how individual a matter the pleasures or pain of retirement may be, a person's response to retired life is influenced by her or his social surroundings—family, friends, neighborhood, and the overall atmosphere in the society. In this chapter we focus on two issues: (1) whether being embedded in a network of social relationships affects the way people experience retired life, and (2) how the retired role is influenced by broad social, economic, and political trends.

Social Networks: Family, Friends, Community

It has long been recognized that social ties—to family, friends, or community—help the individual deal with the stresses of life. Research attests to the importance of social bonds in helping to protect people from suicide and ill health, reducing complications of pregnancy, cushioning the effect of unemployment, easing the impact of divorce, and helping the sick to recover

(Cobb, 1979; Durkheim, 1951; Kahn, 1979; Liem & Liem, 1978). Social support takes many forms: letting others know that they are loved and esteemed and that help is available, if needed; taking care of those who need such care; and providing goods, services, and advice. In other words, giving aid and encouragement, affirming the individual's worth, and offering comfort and affection. In general, being part of a supportive network helps people to cope and maintain emotional stability. We should expect, then, that those retirees who are married and who have social contacts with family, friends, and neighbors have an advantage in dealing with the changes that accompany retirement.

Close and Intimate Relationships

Consider marriage: for people of all ages, one of the most important functions of the modern family is to provide emotional support to family members. During the working years, the family ideally serves as a haven from the stresses of work. During the retirement years—again, ideally—marital partners provide companionship to each other and help ease the difficulties of making the transition from work to retirement.

Whether marriages actually function in retirement according to the ideal model is not clear. Among older people in general there is a slight positive relationship between marital status and subjective well-being, independent of socioeconomic status (Larson, 1978). Results from the few studies that deal specifically with the relationship between marital status and satisfaction with retirement are not straightforward. For example, there are some hints that the never-married have as high morale as the married retirees; it is the divorced, separated, and widowed who are most likely to be unhappy (Barfield & Morgan, 1970; see also Larson, 1978). Perhaps the never-married prefer the single state or have long since accommodated to it. But the dissatisfactions of those whose marriages have been disrupted by death or divorce merely underscore the importance of marriage. There are also clues that marital status, in itself, has little effect on older women's morale (J. H. Fox, 1977; see also Larson, 1978). Finally, we know little about the quality of the marital relationships of retirees, whether they change after retirement, and how the character of the marital relationship affects retired life. All such qualifications aside, in our opinion the balance of available evidence suggests that marriage is beneficial to most retirees.

Whatever contribution marriage makes to the morale of retired persons, retirement itself may create new problems for the married retiree and her or his spouse. Retirement often disrupts familiar role patterns, requiring both husband and wife to make adjustments. Just getting used to being together all day creates problems in some families. One husband complains that since he and his wife have no interests in common, retirement has brought more strain to the marriage than when they were both employed. A retired woman notes that no matter how congenial a married couple may be, the change of schedule curtails privacy (Ingraham, 1974).

One of the most common changes in the family that accompanies retirement is an alteration in the division of labor. Retired husbands tend to participate more in household tasks than when they were working. In many retired families both husband and wife enjoy the new family togetherness (Riley & Foner, 1968). But in other families these rearrangements cause difficulties. Traditionally, husbands are usually less experienced and skillful than wives at household tasks. Some of the retired men resent taking orders from their wives about how chores should be done. One retired man told interviewers that the thing he least liked about retirement was working under orders in what he called "Honey do jobs" (Ingraham, 1974). Another man who had been a top executive in a large firm noted in a newspaper interview that when he was in business and said "Jump!" $30,000-a-year employees jumped. "Now, I go home, I walk in the door and my wife says, 'Milton, take out the garbage.' I never saw so much garbage." (Quigley, 1979, p. 9). His solution, by the way, was to get out of the house and work in the Executive Volunteer Corps, a volunteer agency in a nearby city.

For some families—more often in working-class than in middle-class families—these changes in husband's household performance violate deeply held values about the proper sphere of each sex: that the husband should be the provider and perhaps engage in "outside" chores, and that the wife should take care of the children and the home. After retirement, willy-nilly, husbands are drawn into work that many of them consider to be "woman's work." Husbands believing in strict segregation of tasks by sex often find the home chores they do demeaning (Troll, 1971); wives with similar attitudes are not likely to welcome their husbands' encroachment on what the women consider their domain.

Still another problem is likely to confront increasing numbers of retired couples. With labor force participation rates of married women climbing, and with more and more women working full-time for most of their adult lives, husbands and wives will be increasingly concerned about how to mesh their retirement plans. The problem is exacerbated by the age gap between the typical husband and wife, most men being at least a few years older. In the past most married working women seem to have shaped their retirement plans around those of their husbands (Streib & Schneider, 1971). As increasing numbers of women develop strong work commitments, it is likely that more women will want to keep working after their husbands retire, or at least not retire early. Some women will remain working in order to qualify for full pension and social security benefits on their own. Signs of such a trend have already been observed. In 1974, among retired married men aged 63–69, 46% of their wives already received or were likely to receive in the future retired benefits on their own. That is, the wives had worked for a sufficiently long period of time to qualify or be likely to qualify for benefits on the basis of their own work records. Among couples where both had been employed, many did not retire together; almost one-third of the wives whose husbands had retired at 65–69 had not yet retired themselves (A. Fox, 1979).

We can only speculate about how married couples will react to situations where one of them is retired and the other continues to work. Consider the problems in families where it is the wife who remains in the labor force. Prior to retirement, in most dual-job families, wives still had the major responsibility for household tasks. For example, one study found that only 4% of the men but 44% of the women in dual-worker families put in more than three and a half hours a day on household chores on work days. On weekends, 53% of the men and 82% of the women said they did more than three and a half hours of housework (Bennetts, 1979).

If the husband retires while the wife continues to hold a job, one possible rearrangement of the household division of labor is a role reversal, with retired husbands having the major responsibility for housekeeping tasks and the wife helping out as she has time. Husbands who undertake full household management may have few "hang-ups" about the proper sphere of men and women, but we would expect that being "only a househusband" would cause difficulties even for these men—if only because most of them will not have had a lifetime of experience in developing skills in the household arts. However, it seems unlikely that most retired husbands will willingly assume full responsibility for running the home. Thus, in many families working women will continue to do what most of them had done before their husbands retired—retain their combined roles of homemaker and worker. Whereas these women may have accepted a double burden when their husbands were working, they are likely to resent their husbands' not taking on more household tasks after retirement. We suspect that most families where wives continue to hold a job after the husband has retired will steer a middle course between the two extremes of complete role reversal in the household division of labor and husband's nonparticipation in home duties. Whatever arrangements are made, there are likely to be new tensions in marital relationships.

Marriage is not the only important relationship that retirees have. Retirees maintain, and possibly increase, contact with their children, grandchildren, and other kin (see Chapter 3). Apparently, such family relationships play a central role (Friedmann & Orbach, 1974). At the same time, both retirees and their children prefer to maintain some independence between generations; and such independence is associated with high morale among retirees (Kerckhoff, 1966; Riley & Foner, 1968). Retirees often cherish their privacy; they also understand that "the children have their own lives to live."

Contacts with children are important, but there are indications that these contacts with children and other relatives may be a mixed blessing. One set of research has come up with the intriguing finding that visits with children may have a depressing rather than an uplifting effect on older (65 +) male retirees (Dowd & LaRossa, 1978; see also Bell, 1976). Dowd and LaRossa suggest that this apparently negative effect of visits with children occurs because power relationships in the family change when older men retire. Retired men have to cede a measure of control to their adult children, a process that undoubtedly occurs quite subtly. Visiting with children serves to emphasize such changed relationships. (See Hess & Waring, 1978 for a discussion of potential strains between middle-aged children and their parents.)

Other research analyzes the association between life satisfaction and frequency of contact with relatives (relationship not specified). At least among middle-class and upper-middle-class retirees who were soon to move to a leisure village, there was no relationship between morale and contacts with relatives. That is, seeing relatives did not have negative consequences, but it apparently did not contribute to these retirees' sense of well-being either (Lemon, Bengtson, & Peterson, 1972).

The point we want to stress is that while marital and family relationships are an important source of emotional and instrumental support for retirees, these relationships themselves are bound to be affected by retirement. As retirement leads to rearrangements in family roles, family relationships are subject to new strains.

Interaction with friends and neighbors is another significant resource for retirees and often serves to complement kinship networks. Friendly relations may be less emotionally tinged than relationships within the family. Friends provide a welcome ear for confidences; they are company for social and leisure activities. Friends and neighbors are a source of mutual assistance. They look in on one another; they help out when someone is sick; they do errands; they lend (or they borrow); and they give advice and listen to complaints, and the like. Whether contacts with neighbors specifically contribute to overall morale is not clear. Seeing friends and having a confidant does seem to be important for the person's morale (J. H. Fox, 1977; Lemon et al., 1972; Lowenthal & Haven, 1968). In this latter respect men are at a disadvantage. Older men are less likely than older women to have close relationships with friends or to have a confidant (Booth, 1972; Lowenthal & Haven, 1968). These findings bring to mind studies we discussed above that found no relationship between marital status and morale among older women. Perhaps because women have more intimate friendships than men do, older women depend less on marital relationships for emotional support.

The Residential Environment

Since at least some kinds of social contacts are important for the morale of retired people, what types of residential environment are most likely to foster such contacts? For example, does retirement housing, with its high concentration of older people, provide the most favorable environment for maintaining social ties?

Retirement housing has proliferated as the proportion of older people in the population has grown. Yet the current residents of retirement housing tend to be a small and unrepresentative sample of the older population (Carp,

1976). What has been termed "retirement housing" encompasses a variety of living arrangements, ranging from relatively affluent retirement communities to low-cost publicly supported facilities, from enclaves of one-family homes to highrise apartments. Leisure facilities may be luxurious or simple.

People living in retirement housing have relatively high rates of social interaction (Carp, 1976). When residents of several types of retirement housing are compared to residents of dispersed and age-integrated housing—matched for age, sex, socioeconomic status, working status, marital status, number of children, tenure, and household composition—those living in retirement housing report more new friends, more visits with friends who are age peers, and more visits with neighbors. At the same time, they have less contact with their children than those living in age-heterogeneous housing. Residents of retirement housing are not neglected by their children, however. Their children are there when the older parents need them, and the parents often assist the children. Thus, as with residents of dispersed housing, there is a pattern of mutual assistance between older people and their children (Susan R. Sherman, 1975a, 1975b). Whether living in retirement housing contributes to morale is unclear. Since the term "retirement housing" is somewhat of a misnomer—residents include widows who have never worked for pay, older people who are in the labor force, and housewives as well as retired people—the few studies that deal with the impact of retirement housing do not focus on the effect of the residential environment on retirees specifically.

What about the vast majority of retirees who live in dispersed and age-integrated settings? They not only maintain contact with their children, but also with friends and neighbors. One reason for this is that older people tend to stay put and long-term residence is associated with having social ties in the neighborhood. True, retired people are more likely to move than older people who are not retired. But census data on residential mobility over a five-year period indicate that even among the retired only a minority moved their residence and most of this moving was within county lines. Second, a high proportion of older people are home-owners, and owners are more likely than renters to have community and neighborhood ties (Riley & Foner, 1968). Further, many retired people, especially those in good health and with economic resources, are not circumscribed by their neighborhood for social contacts. Indeed, health and socioeconomic status are probably more important than type of housing in influencing the social life of retirees. While those in good health and with adequate economic resources can transcend their immediate residential environment to maintain social contacts, those with few resources are particularly vulnerable to the shortcomings of their surroundings—as are inner city residents of deteriorating neighborhoods or residents of isolated rural areas.

In sum, the residential environment is important to older people in many ways. For example, older people want comfortable, clean, and safe homes, and they like to be close to shops, services, and public transportation. Older people's homes can keep them busy with cleaning, laundering, and gardening chores. At the same time their homes may need costly repairs which only some older people can manage by themselves. With inflation and energy problems, heating homes often overtaxes budgets. Whether these physical and financial aspects of their housing are related to their overall morale is not known (Carp, 1976).

Since social ties are linked to retirees' subjective well-being, we have focused here specifically on the influence of the residential environment on opportunities for social contacts. Retirees in many different kinds of residential settings are able to maintain ties to family, friends, and neighbors. Older people's homes are frequently social centers for their relatives and friends who come to visit, play cards, and share meals, and for children and grandchildren who may come to stay overnight. However, those with meager resources, who typically depend on their immediate neighborhood for social contacts, are often in settings that offer meager chances for a meaningful social life. Needless to say, the housing of those with limited incomes is likely to be less comfortable in other ways. Thus, we return to a familiar theme: the importance of economic and other resources. In the following pages, we will find that the impact of economic and political trends in the whole society on the retired person's economic well-being is a key issue.

The Societal Environment

In the early decades of this century, people thought that retirement was appropriate only for those who were physically unable to work. As recently as 1950, in a sample of steel workers age 55 and over, more than half of them felt this way, while only one-quarter thought of retirement as a reward for a lifetime of work, and fewer than 30% said it was a well-earned rest. Just ten years later, in 1960, older workers in the same company had quite different views: less than 25% said retirement was only for the physically impaired; two-thirds thought of it as a reward for a lifetime of work; and about 45% thought of it as a well-earned rest (Ash, 1966). Marked changes in attitude toward retirement have taken place even more recently. In 1974, 43% of a national sample of adult employees said they personally looked forward to retirement. By 1978, this proportion had gone up to 54%. Interestingly, in 1978, 63% of those on the threshold of retirement (age 50–64) said they looked forward to retirement (Harris, 1979). In general, before the 1950s there was a fairly widespread opposition to retirement; by the mid-1960s, American studies were consistently reporting a favorable outlook toward retirement, especially among manual workers and many categories of white-collar workers, provided they had an adequate income (Friedmann & Orbach, 1974).

As we have seen, this trend has continued well into the 1970s. Within the past 30 years, then, there has been a revolution in attitudes toward retirement. These dramatic changes in views of retirement reflect important economic, political, and social changes in the whole society.

The Economic and Political Climate

Probably the most important factor affecting workers' attitudes about retirement is economic. As noted previously, concern with income is a key influence on early retirement and on satisfaction with retirement. Prior to the mid-1930s, the only workers who could afford to retire were those who had considerable savings. The few public and private pension programs that were in effect then had strict eligibility requirements and were often tied to impaired work capacity. Most private employers reserved the company's right to discontinue payment of benefits at any time (Achenbaum, 1978). The 1935 Social Security Act broke this tradition; it established the right of most workers to a pension at age 65. Since the establishment of the social security system, there has been a significant expansion of coverage so that all but a small minority of the regular work force are covered. Not only has coverage expanded, but the average social security benefit paid to a retired worker has increased, and benefit increases tied to the cost of living have been legislated in the past decade. In fact, during the first part of the 1970s (from 1970 to 1973), increases in benefits were more than enough to offset price increases (Hollister, 1974). (Chapter 7 discusses details of the social security system more fully.)

In addition to social security, increasing numbers of retirees are receiving private pension benefits. In 1967, only 20% of retired households were receiving two pensions (Atchley, 1976). According to the Retirement History Study, among those who stopped working between 1968 and 1972, 31% of the nonmarried women, 43% of the nonmarried men, and 52% of the married men were receiving dual pensions (A. Fox, 1976; see also Chapter 3 for data on retired population as a whole). And, as mentioned previously, those with dual pensions have higher incomes than those who have only social security benefits.

These income maintenance programs are the major underpinnings of the economic welfare of older people. There are other significant programs as well. Medicare provides for coverage of a good part of older people's medical costs—for example, the bulk of in-patient hospital care and, through Medicare medical insurance, part of the bills for doctors and other medical services. There have been federal and state tax benefits; property tax relief laws, exemptions from sales tax on prescription drugs, a double personal exemption for federal taxes, and exclusion from capital gains tax of gains from sale of personal residence (Schulz, 1976). There are also various discounts for older people, like those in public transportation. All these programs have enabled many retirees to maintain a modest standard of living, with some retirees experiencing no curtailment in their style of life. This is not to say that such programs meet the financial needs of all retired people. Those who have been retired for a long time and those living on social security payments alone are particularly likely to be economically disadvantaged; many of these retirees fall below the poverty line (see Chapter 3).

Whatever the deficiencies in public and private programs for the retired, we suggest that these programs have helped to solidify favorable attitudes toward retirement. It is not only that these programs have served to alleviate the financial worries of many retirees, but also that public policies have served to legitimize retirement. The relationship between public policy and attitudes is, of course, debatable. We believe that whether or not favorable public attitudes helped to initiate social welfare programs for the aged in the first place, these programs for the retired are now extensive and put the public stamp of approval on older workers' right to retire. There is little doubt that the public feels those who choose to retire or who are no longer able to work should have the right to retire and to turn to the government for financial support. In a 1974 survey the vast majority of the general public expressed such sentiments; moreover, a very high percentage of the public feels that the government should provide older, retired people with enough income to live comfortably (Harris, 1975).

Social Context

The expansion of income maintenance programs has, of course, been an important factor in the dramatic increase in the proportion of older workers who have retired. The sheer number of retirees in our society in itself has an important, if subtle, effect on attitudes toward retirement. As more and more people have retired, retiring has come to be seen as what people do in later years. As the retired population has grown, a large network of organizations and services has sprung up. Businesses have come to recognize the importance of the retiree market. For example, builders of retirement housing and travel and leisure industries actively solicit the patronage of retired persons. Inducements offered by businesses to the 65-and-over population in general also benefit retirees. Thus, they can take advantage of consumer products and services now being packaged to meet the special needs of older people. Retirees can go to the local movie houses, restaurants, pharmacies, or beauty parlors that offer discounts to older people.

The past several decades have seen the proliferation and growth of organizations for retirees. There are a few mass membership organizations like the National Retired Teachers Association and the American Association of Retired Persons claiming a combined dues-paying membership in 1979 of over 11 million. A main function of the NRTA–AARP is to provide insurance for retired persons. The organization also offers other services such as home-delivery pharmacy service; eligibility for group health insurance; discount privileges at leading hotel, motel, and rent-a-car chains; free assistance on taxes; temporary employment placement services in many urban areas; and group tours.

Numerous smaller groups also provide a variety of services to retired members and are attracting increasing numbers. For example, in the 1950s less than 10% of older people generally attended local, special clubs and centers for older persons (Riley & Foner, 1968). By the 1970s almost 20% of older people reported they participated to some extent in senior centers and the like; one-half of the older people said that there was such a center fairly nearby (Harris, 1975). One of the attractions of many of these centers is a free lunch that can be shared with other older people; free lunches and sometimes free transportation are supported by federal funds. Undoubtedly retirees are among those benefitting from these expanded programs. But there are also clubs specifically for retirees. One such organization is the local club organized around former employees of particular firms. Many trade unions now also have extensive programs for retired members. They provide social services and offer recreational, cultural, and political activities to members. One local union, for example, arranges for personal visits to all members who have just retired. Another local union has current events discussion groups, political action groups, and photography workshops; it arranges day trips to nearby museums or other places of interest, and encourages participation in the creative arts and attendance at cultural events.

The clubs and organizations described above offer services to retirees; there are also programs (many of which are stimulated and supported by the federal government) that provide opportunities for retirees to serve others. For example, ACTION, the federal volunteer agency, supports the following programs:

- *Foster Grandparents*. This program offers opportunities to low-income men and women 60 and over and in good health to provide attention and care to physically, emotionally, and mentally handicapped children in institutions and in private settings. Foster grandparents work four hours a day, five days each week, devoting two hours a day to each of two children in their care. They feed and dress the child, play games and read stories, or help with speech and physical therapy. Volunteers receive training and are supervised by child-care teams; they receive a stipend and a transportation allowance, hot meals while in service, accident insurance, and annual physical examinations.
- *Senior Companions*. This program is patterned after Foster Grandparents, except that volunteers provide services to adults with special needs.
- *Retired Senior Volunteer Program*. RSVP offers retired men and women 60 and over a chance to serve in a variety of organizations and institutions such as courts, schools, hospitals, libraries, day-care centers, nursing homes, Boy Scout and Girl Scout offices, economic development agencies, and other community service centers. Volunteers teach children to read, tutor boys and girls on probation, visit the elderly in nursing homes, do clerical work in hospitals, make daily phone calls to housebound people, and even sing to hospital patients.
- *The Service Corps of Retired Executives*. SCORE is a volunteer program that links retired businessmen and women who have management expertise with the owners or managers of small businesses in need of management counseling. Volunteers have helped grocery and drug stores, restaurants, hardware stores, repair shops, dry cleaners, clothing stores, truckers, and

the like. They have helped steer some people away from businesses that were extremely risky or for which the potential owners had too little experience or capital. SCORE is cosponsored by ACTION and the Small Business Administration.

In addition to these programs, retirees have opportunities to offer their services in programs involving people of all ages. VISTA (Volunteers in Service to America) accepts people of all ages with particular talents and experience who work for a minimum of one year in impoverished urban and rural areas. The Peace Corps actively recruits older people to serve a minimum of two years as overseas volunteers helping developing nations with such programs as agriculture, mathematics and science teaching, teacher training, manpower training and vocational trades, business and public administration, and natural resource development and conservation. ACTION Cooperative Volunteers is for people of all ages who wish to contribute one year of service to local projects that help communities tackle problems of poverty and the environment.

This brief survey indicates that there are many opportunities for retirees to engage in stimulating and meaningful activities, to have social contacts with age peers, and to participate in programs that are socially useful. And the fact that retirees are a target group for business and the special organizations mentioned above serves to legitimate and enhance the position of retirees in society.

Finally, with so many retirees in the population, the isolation of retirees from each other is reduced. The large number of retirees in the population means that even the majority who do not live in retirement housing or participate in special programs run for and by retirees in schools, unions, churches and synagogues, or voluntary agencies are likely to come into contact with other retirees. Perhaps they meet at the store when they go for the paper; or perhaps they run into one another when they walk their dogs or when they work on cars or do gardening and yard work. As retirees are thrown into each other's company or hear about each other, they learn from one another and develop their own norms about what is appropriate behavior in retirement. Even if they don't have much contact with other retirees, they are likely to hear about other people who are retired and what these other retirees are doing. The size of the retired population, then, provides an environment for people to shape the retirement role collectively. Further, the size of the retired population enhances the visibility of retired people as a group. This increased visibility means that there are more role models than ever before for those on the threshold of retirement.

Conclusion

Factors beyond the individual are crucial to understanding general attitudes toward retirement and how retired persons respond to their role. Family, friends, and neighborhoods provide emotional and instrumental support that helps the individual cope with this new role. Just as important, but less tangible, are the broad societal trends that have served to redefine the retirement role as an earned right; the increasing number of retired people that makes it possible for retirees to provide peer support to each other; the burgeoning number of organizations and services that are attracting retirees; and above all, the public and private programs that provide income maintenance and underwrite needed services.

In this regard, economic conditions in the future seem critical. We have already speculated on the possible impact of inflation on plans for early retirement. Continued inflation is likely to affect the economic welfare of those who have actually retired. Retirees who depend on social security benefits alone are protected from inflation to some extent, since increases in their benefits have been tied to the cost of living. But these people have little enough in the first place. Private pension funds are not geared to the cost of living or protected against inflationary trends, for the most part. To be sure, private pension benefits have increased; but the increases have not kept up with increases in the cost of living (G. B. Thompson, 1978b). Ironically, retirees with dual pensions who have been better off in the past than those depending on social security alone may feel the pinch of inflation more sharply than these other retirees, at least in relative terms. Most retirees have only very modest financial assets like money in the bank, stocks and bonds, or mutual funds. Most retirees own their own homes and the majority of these homeowners have paid off their mortgages; yet the advantage of homeownership is counterbalanced by rising costs of home maintenance. It is not surprising, then, that inflationary trends threaten the economic well-being of many retirees. In 1978, 42% of retirees claimed that inflation had seriously reduced their standard of living; another 42% said their standard of living was reduced somewhat by inflation (Harris, 1979). Given the importance of an adequate income to older people's feelings about life in retirement, if inflation continues unabated, the high levels of satisfaction with retirement found in the past two decades may well decline.

Such changes in the economic conditions of the society suggest the reaction of present generations of retirees may not be a reliable guide to the way future cohorts of retirees will respond to retirement. It is not only economic conditions that may change; we already know of other trends that are certain to make the character of new cohorts of retirees quite different from that of earlier cohorts. For example, the educational level of future retirees will be higher on the average than that of today's retirees. These better-educated retirees may expect more of retirement than retirees with lower educational attainment. Or to take another trend that has emerged in the 1970s, future retirees more than today's retirees will have been exposed to intensive public educational programs on the importance of good nutrition and regular exercise. Retirees who have adhered to healthful regimens may be more capable and more disposed than today's retirees to engage in wide-ranging activities, including sports and tasks requiring physical stamina. We may well wonder if future retirees will be attracted to programs like Foster Grandparents; whether they will want federally underwritten breakfasts and lunches in community facilities (Waring, 1978). The changing character of new cohorts of retirees poses new problems for public policy just as economic and demographic trends have confronted policy makers with new challenges. In the next chapter we discuss some of the new difficulties associated with retirement facing the society.

Review Questions
for Chapter 6

1. *What problems does retirement pose for married couples? Do you think these problems affect satisfaction with retirement? Satisfaction with married life in retirement? What kind of research is needed to answer these questions?*
2. *Discuss sex differences in social relationships of retired persons. What do you think are the reasons for these differences?*
3. *Do you think that attitudes to retirement in the future will be the same as they are now? If so, why? If not, why? If not, why do you think they will change, and in what way do you expect them to change?*

7

Retirement
Policy
in a
Changing
Society

A major thread running through our analysis of retirement is the crucial role of social security in the United States. The establishment and subsequent expansion of the social security system is one of the key factors associated with the growing number of retirees in our society, with the trend toward early retirement, and with retirees' satisfaction with retired life. Changes the system faces are thus likely to have wide repercussions.

It is no wonder then that potential problems in the social security system have received widespread attention. For the past few years "scare" headlines and newspaper stories have warned that the social security system in the United States is in trouble. Actually, some newspaper and magazine articles have exaggerated the extent of the difficulties faced by the program. As noted in our introductory chapter, there is *no* danger that the social security system will "go broke"; there are any number of methods of financing pension benefits that would assure the solvency of the system, although each method has some drawbacks. But just as the system changed in the past, it is subject to further alterations because the society itself is changing. In this chapter we will try to understand the impact of demographic, economic, and social changes on public retirement policy. We will sketch briefly the history of the social security system in the United States; discuss the trends that have influenced the growth of the system, created current dilemmas, and are likely to give rise to problems in the future; and explore alternative solutions to these problems.

The U. S. Social Security System: How It Grew

The social security system in the United States was established in 1935 in the depths of the Great Depression. It was designed as a contributory wage-related plan. That is, it was to be financed by payments from both the worker and the employer. Benefits were to be paid according to the employee's record of earnings; the amount of money paid into the social security fund by and for each worker to be kept on record so that the individual's retirement benefits could be properly determined. It may now be hard to believe that in those troubled times, when about one-quarter of the labor force was out of work, many people thought that a government old-age social insurance plan would destroy people's incentives to work and to save. Thus, the notion that the mainstay of the program was to be the prospective retiree's own contributions—and that of her or his employer—was politically critical. Because the plan provided that benefits would be tied to the individual's own work history, the original policymakers felt that the program would win approval from Congress. In addition, the fact that social security financing sounded like other insurance plans—but with the backing of the United States government—gave the public a sense of entitlement into the system and a feeling that they would get "their" benefits when they retired (Manney, 1975).

Of course, as we know, the social security program is not like other insurance schemes whereby the individual puts money away for the future. Early in the history of the program—even before the first benefits were paid in 1940—its funding was put on a pay-as-you-go basis, with a **social security trust fund** set up primarily as a safety cushion in case of economic adversity ("Propping Up Social Security," 1976). Thus, in effect, current social security tax receipts pay for current benefits. Such funding is not unique to the United States; it is characteristic of many major social security systems throughout the world. One reason for this type of funding in the United States was that meaningful pensions could not be paid in the first years of the program if pensions were to be based mainly on retirees' contributions and those of their employers. Later on, this pay-as-you-go financing made it possible to broaden coverage and increase benefits.

When the social security program was first initiated, only workers in commerce and industry were covered; among those who were excluded were farm workers, the self-employed, private household employees, and workers in nonprofit institutions, a large proportion of whom were hospital workers in voluntary, nonprofit hospitals. At its inception, the basic **social security payroll tax** was only 1% each for the employee and the employer. The tax applied to the first $3000 of annual earned income; thus, the maximum contribution a worker could make was $30 a year. The **benefit base** of $3000 a year seems quite low to us now; but then it was quite inclusive since at that time the vast majority of workers (97%) earned $3000 a year or less.

Since the establishment of the social security system in the United States, the program has changed in a number of ways. Close to 95% of all workers now have social security coverage. Many other workers are covered by public employee retirement programs. Although social security taxes have gone up over the years, so have benefits. The benefit base (the portion of earnings subject to payroll taxes) has also been raised; in 1980, workers paid social security taxes on the first $25,900 of earnings. Even so, there were still highly paid employees (earning $26,000 a year or more) who had a portion of their earnings untaxed.

Not only has the number of workers covered by social security increased, but the kinds of benefits paid out have expanded. The initials OASDHI tell the story. Benefits are paid to retirees (old age), survivors and dependents of covered workers, disabled workers, and the aged and disabled for hospital and some other medical expenses under the Medicare program. To sum up the key provisions of the social security system:

- Employers and employees both pay social security taxes on the employee's earnings below the taxable maximum. In 1979–1980, the tax rate paid by each was 6.13%; it was to go up to 6.65% in 1981 and 6.70% in 1982–1984. The maximum amount of annual earnings that could be taxed was $25,900 in 1980, scheduled to go up to $29,700 in 1981.
- To receive benefits, workers must have worked for a minimum period of time on a covered job (with the exact period of time required for eligibility depending on the year person became 21).[1] The amount of benefits workers receive is tied to past earnings.
- Individuals can receive retired-worker benefits before age 65—as early as age 62—but if they do, their benefits are reduced. Workers who delay receiving benefits until after age 65 receive a bonus of 1% for each year they delay. In 1982 this bonus will go up to 3%.
- Eligible wives and children receive a portion of the basic benefit, while widows 65 and over receive the full benefits to which the worker was entitled.
- Individuals receiving retired-worker benefits can continue to work, but if their earnings exceed the amounts specified in the "**earnings test**," their benefits are reduced. For example, in 1980 people aged 65 and older who

[1]To be eligible for retired-worker benefits, a person who turned 21 before 1950 must have earned $50 or more in covered employment in a calendar quarter for each year that elapsed after 1950 up to the year he or she reaches age 62. To be fully insured, a person aged 62 in 1979 must have worked in covered employment for 28 quarters or the equivalent of 7 years. Workers reaching age 21 in 1950 or later need 40 quarters of coverage to be fully insured (Mallan & Cox, 1978).

earned more than $5000 had their benefits reduced. By 1982 this "exempt" amount will rise to $6000. Retired workers 72 and older get full benefits no matter how much they earn; by 1982 the "exempt" age will be 70.

The Social Security Administration also has the responsibility for administering the Supplementary Security Income (SSI) program, which went into effect in 1974. SSI replaced many state-administered assistance programs that provided relief for the elderly poor, blind, and disabled. SSI in 1979 guaranteed a minimum annual income of $3747.60 for eligible couples 65 and over and $2498.40 for eligible aged individuals. A number of states supplement the minimum income provided by SSI.

Table 7-1 gives some idea of the size of the social security program today, the number of persons receiving benefits (beneficiaries), and the total payments made. At the end of May, 1979, for example, the OASDI program paid over $8 billion in monthly benefits to about 35 million beneficiaries, exclusive of Medicare and SSI payments (*Social Security Bulletin*, September 1979).

TABLE 7-1. Monthly OASDI Benefits, May 1979

Total monthly beneficiaries (in thousands)	34,815
Aged 65 and over, total	22,743
Retired workers	16,630
Survivors and dependents	5,988
Special age-72 beneficiaries	124
Under age 65, total	12,072
Retired workers	1,912
Disabled workers	2,878
Survivors and dependents	7,282
Total monthly benefits (in millions)	$8,057
Average benefit in current payment status[a]	
Retired workers	265.16
Disabled workers	290.80
Aged widows and widowers	241.32
Children of deceased workers	183.95

[a]Excludes lump-sum and retroactive payments and adjustments.

Adapted from *Social Security Bulletin*, 1979, p. 1.

The amount of money distributed by the social security system in the United States seems quite impressive. These expenditures can be put into perspective by comparing outlays in the United States to other modern, industrial countries. One measure that is used for international comparisons is the proportion of *Gross National Product* (GNP) spent on social security. GNP is a measure of the total goods and services produced in a country. Studies indicate that other countries spend a greater portion of their GNP for pensions than the United States does. In part this is because several of these countries have a higher proportion of older people in their population. But some countries (Sweden and The Netherlands, for example) devote a higher proportion of their GNP to outlays for all types of social welfare programs, many of which benefit older people (Merriam, 1978).

Even though other countries have more comprehensive social welfare policies than we do, social security in the United States is vital to the economic welfare of most older people. Social security is the major source of income for many retirees; 56% of all older married couples and 73% of older non-married people receive half or more of their income from social security (Grad & Foster, 1979). In the relatively brief period of time since the Social Security Act was passed, social security has become a central method by which Americans finance their retirements.

Emerging Problems: The Financial Squeeze

How has it been possible for the social security program in the United States to grow, to pay increasing benefits, and to peg benefits to the cost of living in recent years? An important part of the explanation lies in favorable economic conditions in the society. Financial problems the system now faces are in part the result of the changing economic context.

Not only in the United States, but throughout the industrialized world, there was an almost uninterrupted expansion of social security in the 1960s, and in some countries even through the early 1970s. For example, France extended social security coverage to include students, the handicapped, and non-wage earners; Germany, Norway, and Sweden introduced flexible retirement; Belgium and Italy introduced income maintenance for the poor by a means-tested guaranteed income (Fisher, 1978). Such an expansion was made possible by increasing productivity and full employment. In the United States, for example, the number of persons of working age increased, thus providing a growing tax base to support retirees. Economic growth helped to raise hourly rates of pay and thus added to social security revenues (Kreps, 1976).

But this prosperous economic picture was clouded in the 1970s. On the one hand, a slump in employment reduced social security revenues; on the other hand, inflation led to increased outlays, since benefits were tied to the cost of living. Also serving to erode reserve funds in the United States was the trend toward early retirement that not only increased the social security load but reduced the contributions to the social security fund.

Faced with the potential depletion of the social security reserve fund, measures were adopted in the United States in 1977 to shore up the financial soundness of the program. Benefits were still kept up-to-date with increases in prices, but the 1977 legislation enacted a new benefit formula that resulted in benefit levels for new retirees (in 1979 and after) about 5% lower than those expected to prevail in 1979 under the old law.[2] The new law also provided for increases in the contribution of employees and employers and a rise in the amount of the individual's annual earnings that can be taxed (Snee & Ross, 1978).

The approach taken in the United States to assure the financial stability of the social security system is but one possible method of dealing with the problems of reduced revenues and increased benefits. Before considering other methods, let us examine yet another difficulty for the system that looms in the future.

Emerging Problems: The Demographic Squeeze

The method of financing retirement benefits under social security makes the system sensitive not only to economic conditions but also to changes in the ratio of workers to retirees. The problem for the future is that the number of beneficiaries per worker is expected to increase markedly by the first quarter of the next century. As the number of retirees expands relative to the number of workers, the financial burden carried by each worker will increase.

The Aging of the Baby-Boom Cohorts

Let us consider the number of people who will be growing old in the next century. Of special interest is the aging of those outsize birth cohorts of the 1950s. The long-term decline in fertility in the United States was interrupted by the "baby-boom" following World War II; **birthrates** in the United States had been declining steadily from 1800 until that period, but the birthrate shot up from 1946 for the next 15–20 years, producing a bumper crop of babies.[3]

As the baby-boom cohorts have grown older, they have strained social institutions at each step along the way. When they reached school age, they prompted a rapid expansion in the number of classrooms and teachers. Later, they were in good part responsible for the growth of the college population. The baby-boom cohorts are now 16–34 years old. As they have reached working age, they have put pressure on the labor force. Members of these cohorts will be reaching their 60s in the years 2010–2030. When these large cohorts make the transition to retirement, they are likely to place strains on the social

[2]The purpose of the 5% reduction was to offset the unintended overadjustment of benefits since automatic cost-of-living increases were adopted in 1972.

[3]The number of babies born to every 1000 women of childbearing age jumped from 85.9 in 1945 to 101.9 in 1946. This general **fertility rate** proceeded to increase to a peak of 122.7 in 1957. In 1958 the fertility rate started to decline, but it was not until 1965 that it dropped below its 1946 level; by 1976 the birthrate was only 65.7 babies born to every 1000 women of childbearing age.

security system—especially since the number of working-age people per retiree is then expected to be lower than it is now.

The Impact of Low Fertility

What then about the size of the working-age population in the future? The high birthrates that produced the baby-boom cohorts were followed by low birthrates and new, smaller cohorts. If future birthrates in this country continue to be low, the oversized baby-boom cohorts will have to be supported in their retirement by small cohorts of workers. The **worker-to-retiree ratio**—the relative number of working-age people to the number of people 65 and older—thus will depend to a large extent upon future fertility rates.[4] While we do not know what future birthrates will be, we can estimate the effect of different levels of fertility upon the worker-to-retiree ratio. Table 7-2 shows three different projected fertility levels and their effects on the proportion of various age groups in the population in the year 2050. Although the year 2050 seems a long way in the future, the table is still useful in illustrating the relationship between birthrates, the age structure of the population, and the worker-to-retiree ratio. For example, Alternative II uses the theoretical population replacement rate of 2.1 children per woman—a fertility rate that Census officials believe to be in the range of likely future birthrates. Under this alternative, 20% of the population would be 65 and over in 2050 and the number of working-age people available to support one retiree would be 2.70, considerably lower than the worker-to-retiree ratio of 5.15 prevailing in 1979. It is noteworthy that in each of the three projections of ultimate fertility used in Table 7-2, by the middle of the next century working-age people will be responsible for more older people than working-age people today. Further, these high **aged dependency ratios** are likely to emerge earlier than the year 2050—probably around the year 2025 (Board of Trustees, 1980; see also Chen & Chu, 1977).

Table 7-2 brings to light an interesting fact about the number of youth under 20 that will have to be supported in the next century. Using any three of the projected birthrates, the proportion of the population that is 65 and over will increase while the proportion of the young in the population will decline. In other words, low fertility rates lead to a decline in the proportion of young

---

[4]A reduction in fertility is the most important factor contributing to an increase in the *proportion* of older people in the population. A decline in mortality, unless it is confined to older ages and is relatively large, does not change the relative proportion of older people in the population. Between 1900 and 1974, reductions in mortality have been greater at younger ages than at older ages. Because of the relatively low level of mortality among those currently under 50, future reductions in mortality can only occur at the ages above 50. If such substantial reductions do occur—they are not anticipated—they will contribute to the aging of the population—that is, to a higher proportion of older people in the population than exists currently. Immigration tends to reduce the proportion of older people, unless the migrants are concentrated in the older ages. Future net immigration is expected to have only a slight effect on the proportion of people over 65 (U.S. Bureau of the Census, 1978).

TABLE 7-2. Age Structure of the Population and Dependency Ratios in 1979 and 2050 under Three Sets of Economic and Demographic Assumptions

	1979	2050		
		Alternative I	Alternative II	Alternative III
Ultimate fertility (average number of babies born per woman, projected)		2.5	2.1	1.5
Percent of population aged:				
Under 20	32%	32%	26%	16%
20–64	57%	54%	54%	51%
65 and over	11%	15%	20%	33%
Aged dependency ratio[a]	.194	.270	.370	.644
Total dependency ratio[a]	.763	.858	.847	.962
Number of working-age people for each aged person	5.15	3.71	2.70	1.55

[a]The total dependency ratio is based on the number of people under age 20, plus the number of people 65 and over, divided by the number of people of working age, aged 20–64. It provides a rough estimate of the number of people to be supported by those of working age. The aged dependency ratio is the population 65 and over as a ratio to the population 20–64.

Adapted from Board of Trustees, 1980, p. 94.

people in the population and thus to an increase in the proportion of older people. Therefore, in the next century people of working age will be responsible for more older people but for fewer young people under 20. In fact, although the aged dependency ratio will increase, the **total dependency ratio** will not change much over time.

Does this mean that public and private funds now spent for the support of youth can be transferred over to support the aged? Probably not to any great extent. Youth receive a good deal of their support from private funds, from people with a direct stake in them: their parents. In contrast, the elderly rely heavily on social security pensions and other public supports, as we have shown in Chapter 3. Public funds spent for health care provide a dramatic example of age differences in sources of support. In 1977 public funds paid for 67% of the health expenses of people 65 and over, with Medicare and Medicaid accounting for 61%, whereas more than two-thirds of the health expenses of those under 19 were paid by private sources (Gibson & Fisher, 1979). Transferring financial support from youth to the elderly is thus complicated by the different sources of financial support for these two age groups. In addition, even though the number of children will decline, total private expenditures for children will probably not be reduced proportionately; parents are likely to provide their two or three children with more goods and services than would have been possible with a larger family.

What about the transfer of public funds now spent on youth to agencies supporting older people? Social investments in schools and services for youth may be reduced somewhat. But public expenditures for young people are borne principally by state and local governments and they are supported by property, sales and excise, and local income taxes; whereas we know that public expenditures for the aged are predominantly under federal programs and rely heavily on social security taxes. Adjusting public expenditures to the growing number of older people would require a major shift in patterns of taxation (Chen & Chu, 1977).

In short, the future increase in the aged dependency ratio will, in its own right, create problems for the society. In particular, the projected decline in the number of working-age people relative to those of retirement age will put further strains on the social security system.

Financing Social Security

Several proposals to meet the current financial problems of social security and to offset the consequences of the declining worker–retiree ratio expected in the future are being discussed. One recommendation—raising social security taxes—has already been put into effect. Theoretically, these taxes could be raised still further in the years to come. Another alternative is to require or to urge older workers to remain in the labor force beyond age 65. Or, social security benefits could be reduced. Another possibility is financing at least some parts of the social security program out of **general revenue taxes.** Finally, another change in the system that has been proposed is to permit individuals to stay in or leave the social security system at will. As we discuss below, this last proposal is hardly likely to assure the financial viability of the social security system.

Increasing Social Security Taxes

This solution to the present and future financing problems of social security has been the most widely discussed of all alternative methods. As noted above, in 1977 Congress passed a comprehensive revision of the social security tax rate structure that should meet the financial obligations of the program through the year 2025. These revisions include a schedule of social security tax increases.

There are two advantages to this solution: (1) there is an attempt to maintain retirees' standard of living, and (2) retirement would not have to be delayed. But there are disadvantages to raising social security taxes. A major shortcoming is that people in the lower income brackets feel the burden of social security taxes more than those in the higher income brackets. First, only earnings are taxed. This means that asset income, usually accruing to relatively wealthy families rather than to middle- and low-income families, is not subject to the social security tax. Second, social security taxes are not adjusted for the number of dependents of the taxpayer. In fact, none of the deductions available under the income tax system are available to social security taxpayers. Third, wages above the taxable maximum are not taxed. In 1980, for example, workers earning over $25,900 had earnings in excess of that amount exempt from the social security tax. Generally then, the higher the earnings, the lower the proportion of total income that is taxed—in other words, the social security tax tends to be a **regressive tax.**

An example will illustrate. A worker earning $20,000 annually in 1980 and who had five children would pay $1226 in social security taxes, slightly less than the $1587.67 paid by an employee earning $65,000 a year, but with no children. However, the former worker would be paying 6.13% of his or her total earnings in social security taxes, while the higher-paid worker would be paying 2.44%. If the employee with the higher pay also had income from assets, the social security tax formed an even smaller proportion of his or her total income.

The regressivity of the social security tax has been softened in some ways. Since the Tax Reduction Act of 1975, for example, low-income workers with dependent children who maintain a household are eligible for an earned income credit of 10% of the first $4000 of their earnings. For earnings above $4000, the credit is reduced somewhat. In effect, the social security tax is reduced for eligible families with earnings under $4000 and is progressive for eligible families with earnings between $4000 and $8000 a year. But couples without dependent children and unmarried earners are not eligible for the earned income credit. In addition, some argue that the regressive tax is balanced by a relatively long-standing progressive benefit schedule that gives low-income workers a bigger return on their contribution than higher-income workers. However, it has been argued that on the average the poor start working earlier (and thus pay taxes longer than the others) and die earlier (thus receiving benefits for a shorter period). Finally, Congress has raised the maximum amount of earnings that is subject to the social security tax. But even with this increase, there are highly paid workers who have a considerable portion of their earnings untaxed.

Apart from the regressive nature of the social security tax, another disadvantage to raising social security payroll taxes is that they will undoubtedly have to go up beyond the high levels at which they are now fixed. They already take a sizable chunk out of the worker's earnings and constitute an important cost to the employer. By the year 2011 the tax rate is scheduled to go to 7.65%. Consider what high rates mean to both worker and employer: in 1978 a worker earning $15,000 annually paid $907.50 in social security taxes and the employer paid the same amount. Were the employee to earn the same salary in 2011, the employee's and the employer's tax would each be

$1147.50 (in 1978 dollars). In other words, the combined employer and employee tax will increase from 12% of workers' 1978 earnings to 15% of annual earnings in 2011.

Although these taxes may seem high, workers and employers have tolerated considerably higher tax levels in Europe. Table 7-3 shows the tax rate paid by employees and employers on employees' salaries in a number of European countries. In several of the countries shown in the table, the combined payroll tax rate is 50% or more!

TABLE 7-3. *Social Security Taxes*[a] *in Selected European Countries in 1978*

	Employee Tax %	Employer Tax %
France	8.43	35.57
Germany[b]	16.18	17.68
Italy	7.45	45.59
The Netherlands	22.85	26.51
Spain	7.60	44.87
Sweden	0.50	32.0
Switzerland	18.37	7.1
United Kingdom	6.50	10.0

[a]Social security in these countries typically includes programs that are financed outside of social security in the United States, such as workman's compensation and unemployment, and programs not available in the United States, such as national health insurance and children's allowances.

[b]As of January 1977.

Based on unpublished data from the Social Security Administration.

Social security programs are typically more comprehensive in Europe than they are in the United States. They generally include unemployment and worker's compensation, which are available in the United States but are not financed by the social security tax. European social security programs also typically include national health insurance, children's allowances, and other features not available in the United States. In West Germany, for example, the combined payroll tax is approximately 30%, about one-third of which buys a national health insurance plan for everyone, a plan much more comprehensive than the United States Medicare program, which covers only older people (Pierson & Jaroslovsky, 1979).

Because the United States is now experiencing a growth in the proportion of older people that Europe has already experienced, there will be pressures to further increase payroll taxes to meet higher retirement costs. However, much depends on the political climate in the country. Not only low- and middle-income workers, but those with higher incomes and employers—especially those in labor intensive firms—may well raise objections to marked increases in social security taxes. In 1978 only 30% of current and retired employees and 49% of business leaders thought that social security taxes should be increased to keep up with the benefits being paid out (Harris, 1979). The movement in California to limit state spending that resulted in the passage of Proposition 13 has spread to a number of geographical regions in the country. If a political climate that opposes increased taxes and favors constraints on public spending persists, we may not follow the European example of higher payroll taxes, but may choose an alternate route.

Reducing Benefits

Another alternative for coping with the projected financial strains on social security is to allow the income of the elderly to deteriorate. Obviously, this runs counter to social policy of the past several decades that has generally tried to increase the income of the elderly. Reducing benefits promises to lower the standard of living of future retirees and of still surviving present retirees, some of whom are already at or below the poverty level.

Yet there is some disagreement about definitions of poverty. Some feel that these definitions ignore hidden benefits the elderly receive (like tax breaks); however, others feel that these definitions leave out the elderly poor who must live with relatives, or that people in all age categories have "hidden" income. On the surface, it appears that the financial position of older people has improved over the past decades, in large part because of increases in social security benefits and programs, such as Medicare and Supplementary Security Income. Using available definitions of poverty, the proportion of older people who are poor has declined since 1960. Nevertheless, despite the decline in the percentage of poor older people, most analysts agree that the aged *are* poorer, on the average, than adults under 65. The experts also recognize that most retirees experience a considerable reduction in income.

The proposal to reduce pension benefits thus raises the question about the proportion of the retiree's former income that should be replaced by social security and other pension benefits. If it is assumed that the aim of social policy is to allow retirees to purchase a life style comparable to their former one, a related—and difficult—problem is how to determine what replacement levels should be. Retirees can live on something less than the amount they earned when they were working: they no longer need to save for retirement. Most retirees have few debts and no children to fully support. A large number of retirees have mortgage-free homes. Those over 65 receive special tax breaks and are granted discounts on some purchases. Retirees no longer incur work-related expenses such as commuting and special clothing. Yet maintenance costs on retirees' homes go up as they do for everyone else. As the individual ages, there are increased expenditures for illness, even with Medicare.

Even if we could determine what optimum replacement levels should be, policymakers may decide it is necessary to cut social security benefits below these levels. This can be done in various ways. Benefits can be raised more slowly in the future than they have been in the past several years. This would result in benefits replacing a relatively smaller portion of the employee's previous salary. If individuals had sufficient advance notice, some might be able to make up the difference with savings. However, many workers simply cannot save this much.

Another way to cut social security costs would be to eliminate some of the benefits now available. There has been some discussion about whether or not the **wife's benefits** paid to retiring couples should be continued in the future, since so many women are now themselves in the labor force and are therefore not fully dependent on their husbands. The **student beneficiary program** is another part of the program that some have argued should be eliminated. Others have suggested that the **death benefit** be eliminated.

Such cuts will obviously be resisted by the elderly and their dependents. How successful they will be depends in part on their political influence, a point we will discuss at the end of this chapter.

Delaying Retirement Age

A third solution to the future financial strains faced by the social security system is to raise the age at which people can collect retired-worker benefits. Delaying retirement not only reduces costs of supporting the aged, but may also increase social security revenues. Such a solution seems to promise keeping social security taxes at or near their present levels without reducing the living standard of retirees.

However, much would depend on the way such a proposal would be implemented. Raising the age at which workers can collect full benefits from social security would affect benefit levels for early retirees and thus discourage many from retiring early—something that workers have been led to expect was their right. Few individuals could afford to retire early unless adequate benefits were available to them. Another method might be less burdensome: giving older workers more opportunities and incentives to stay in the work force than they now have. New legislation has already moved the permissible age of mandatory retirement to age 70 for most workers. Another example of such an incentive has been built into the 1977 social security legislation: by 1982, workers will get a 3% bonus in their social security checks for every year they work after age 65. Of course, such a proposal assumes that jobs will be available for older workers, and it runs counter to beliefs of many business leaders who feel that retirement permits the more rapid promotion of younger (and ostensibly more competent) workers who might otherwise leave the firm (Sheppard & Rix, 1977). In fact, these authors suggest that one possible consequence of continued labor force participation of older workers might be that younger workers will have to accept a general pattern of less rapid promotion opportunities than they had in the past. Clearly such a solution would create new problems, some of which we may not be able to envision.

Financing Social Security from General Revenues

Still another possible solution to the financial problems of social security is to increase general revenue financing of social security benefits. That is, instead of special payroll taxes financing social security benefits, all or part of these benefits would be paid out of general revenue funds financed in large part by income and corporate taxes. In 1978, a substantial minority of current and retired employees favored such a solution. Forty-seven percent of a national sample felt that all or part of the money required for social security benefits should come from sources other than social security taxes. Interestingly, business leaders did not concur. Only 20% of a national sample of business leaders felt this way; 79% felt that social security benefits should be paid entirely from social security taxes (Harris, 1979).

Critics of general revenue financing feel it would erode the earned-right nature of the program and result in loss of fiscal discipline that the need to rely on earmarked taxes now imposes on Congress. That is, some people are afraid that politicians would give in to demands for higher benefits, particularly in election years, without regard to the long-run financial consequences. Others fear there would be too heavy a drain on general government funds (Fisher, 1978). Alternatively, some argue that general fund subsidies of the social security program would reduce the system's reliance on regressive taxation.

We cannot predict whether general revenue financing will be adopted as a major method of financing social security benefits. What seems more likely (a pattern already adopted in several countries) is that general revenues will be relied on for some contribution to social security. One possibility in the United States is for the social security system, financed by payroll taxes, to provide pensions based on the retiree's previous earnings while a supplementary program, financed out of general revenues, would pay additional benefits to those older workers and others whose social security checks leave them below the poverty line. The SSI program in the United States incorporates such features in its program. According to *Business Week* ("Propping Up Social Security," 1976), the fact that SSI is administered by the Social Security Administration probably has blunted the stigma of welfare for many recipients.

Opting Out of Social Security

The 1978 Harris survey asked whether all workers should be required to be part of the social security system and whether people who work for themselves or a company should be able to decide if they want to be part of the system. Of current employees, 37% said that people should be able to decide, and 32% said that, if they could choose, they would get out (Harris, 1979).

Presumably these employees think that their own social security taxes are too high, or that too great a portion of societal resources are allotted to older people, or that they could do better by investing their own money. However, in the absence of payroll or other taxes, workers would need to support their aged parents directly. In addition, they would have to save enough when they were working to support themselves in their own retirement. Is this a realistic alternative? Not for most people. For example, one expert shows that workers would need to save about one-third of their earnings throughout their work lives in order to pay for their retirement (Jaffe, 1975, reported by Kreps, 1976). That was in 1975. With inflation increasing, people would have to put aside still larger portions of their lifetime earnings to provide for their postretirement income. Nor is it likely that most younger people and the retired themselves would welcome having to support their parents. Older people generally cherish their independence, and the middle generation is oriented more to the needs of their offspring than to their elderly parents (Foner, 1969). Indeed, in the past it was necessary to enact laws to make adult children responsible for elderly parents (Achenbaum, 1978).

On balance, a system of social insurance does better than private plans. Because it is compulsory and has such wide coverage, it is a better buy than private arrangements would be for the vast majority of people. Making social security optional might benefit some high-income people, but it would reduce social security revenues and therefore aggravate financial problems of the system.

The Political Implications

As we have seen, the costs of retirement will increase in our society in the coming years, and each proposal for coping with these increases will involve costs to some segments of the population. Reducing benefits places a burden on the old; raising social security taxes is an imposition on the working-age population and is felt most keenly by those with low and middle incomes; raising the retirement age can be distressful to those in poor health and oppressive jobs who look forward to retiring before age 65; general revenue financing is generally opposed by business and those paying high income taxes; and making social security optional would work to the disadvantage of the poor because it would weaken the social security system on which they rely.

A key question for the future is whether those who feel they are bearing a disproportionate share of the costs of social security or are being deprived of a fair share of the benefits will express their discontent in political action and/or protest, and whether such actions will create sharp political divisions in the country. One possible line of cleavage is that between the well-off and those with moderate and low incomes, between business and labor. Such cleavages already underlie political life in our society; debates about social security provide still another issue dividing these two groups.

Another potential line of cleavage is that between age groups. The young and adult working-age population may feel they are being taxed too heavily for benefits they see going to the older people; and they are concerned that they won't get "theirs" when they retire. For example, a *Wall Street Journal* article quotes a housewife writing to her Congressman: "Our two sons have paid thousands and thousands. . . . They won't get 1/50th of it back" (Pierson & Jaroslovsky, 1979). On their part, the older population is also dissatisfied with what they see as their shrinking income and lower standard of living. An elderly beneficiary in a letter to her Congressman complains: "We have social security aid of just $372.50 a month. We are slowly going under. We started with some savings—when that's gone, what then?" (Pierson & Jaroslovsky, 1979).

As many scholars have pointed out, age conflicts are always present beneath the surface of social life. Children and parents are often at odds. Young and older workers frequently do not see eye to eye. But open, sharp, society-wide struggles between age strata such as the youth revolt of the 1960s are less common. What is the likelihood that complaints such as the ones quoted above will be turned against other age groups?

At present, while some people are airing resentments and fears about social security, there are few indications that these complaints are being directed by people in one age group against people in other age groups. Several factors operate to mute conflicts over social security along age lines. For one thing, there is little evidence that the working-age population is united in its views on social security. Rather, people of working age are divided along ethnic, class, and even age lines. For example, among a national sample of current and retired employees, the lower the income the more likely the individual was to feel that all retirement income should be provided through social security. Or, when current and retired employees are compared with business leaders, employees are more likely to feel that social security benefits should be increased with the cost of living (Harris, 1979). Similarly, in this same survey, business leaders were more disposed to increase social security taxes than employees were, whereas employees were more likely than business leaders to support using other taxes to pay benefits. Such differences along class lines are likely to take precedence over identity with age peers.

A related factor is that members of the working-age population in low- and middle-income categories receive indirect benefits from the social security system, which relieves the younger adults of the major responsibility for taking care of older family members. True, payroll taxes are high, but having to support aged parents could be even more of a burden. Thus, within the lower socioeconomic strata people of working age are not likely to see older people as their political foes on issues involving social security.

As for the retired population, it is an open question whether a movement of the old, such as the Townsend Movement of the 1930s, will emerge. The Townsend Movement started during the Great Depression. It proposed a plan to pay each person over age 60 a pension of $200 a month financed out of a national sales tax. The movement attracted over 1 million members at its peak in 1936; it spread to several thousand local clubs in every state. The movement apparently helped to hasten legislation for security of old people at both the federal and state levels. But it did not remain as a political force. By 1953, it had dwindled to 23,000 members and was engaged primarily in recreational activities (Holtzman, 1954; Hudson & Binstock, 1976).

Currently there are a number of age-based national organizations with large memberships—The American Association of Retired Persons and the National Association of Retired Federal Employees, for example. In addition, there are organizations like the National Council on the Aging that are not primarily membership organizations but do engage in efforts to improve the position of older people. However, these organizations play a limited political role. They have access to elected and appointed officials and attempt to influence debates on issues relevant to old people. They generally do not attempt to mobilize older people as an explicit political force (Hudson & Binstock, 1976; Pratt, 1974).

The elderly population does represent a potential political force. Relatively high proportions of older people vote. Often older people are concentrated in geographic areas where their votes can be decisive. Each new cohort of retirees is better educated than earlier cohorts; and with increasing education there is a greater sense of political efficacy, a belief that one's actions and voice count.

Sometimes this potential becomes an actual political force. A recent example illustrates how the factors mentioned above—residential concentration of old people, high voting rates among the old, and a relatively well-educated older group—came together to influence a decision on school budgets. The *New York Times* (Madden, 1979) reported that voters in a Connecticut school district had rejected a proposed budget to run the public schools for the following year. The large number of negative votes on this proposal coming from the three voting districts that take in nearly 4000 residents of Heritage Village provided the margin of defeat. Heritage Village is an affluent retirement community. At the time of the newspaper report, condominiums there were selling in the $50,000–$100,000 price range. One member of a family buying a unit must be at least 50 years old and no children under 18 are permitted. While the residents of Heritage Village comprise less than half of the school district's eligible voters, Heritage Village residents have high voting turnouts—more than 95% in some national elections. Apparently many residents of Heritage Village opposed the school budget because they felt that they received no benefit; that is, they paid high taxes for schools but did not have any children participating in the educational program.

The political clout demonstrated by older people in Heritage Village involved a local and narrow issue. It would be considerably more difficult to organize a unified movement of older people on a national level, for, like the young, older people are divided along class, religious, and ethnic lines. Further, their orientations to their adult children and their grandchildren may well deflect their motivation to engage in protests that could hurt the younger generation. Nevertheless, the example of the Great Depression reminds us that, under special circumstances of widespread and severe distress, older people can be rallied for political action on a nationwide level.

Conclusion

In summary, we can predict that the social security system will face serious problems in the future. Just how serious, we cannot know for sure. For example, less unemployment and inflation as well as more births and greater productivity could improve the outlook (Pierson & Jaroslovsky, 1979).

We assume, however, that economic conditions are not likely to change markedly in the direction indicated above, and that birth projections are fairly accurate. This means that the social security system will have to make some alterations in its program. We have suggested some of the possible solutions, but we cannot foresee which ones, or which combination of solutions, will be selected. Nor can we foretell all the consequences of such changes. Whatever the shape of the future program of social security, it will have an impact on the whole society and will affect retirees, the working population, the economy, political life, and the relations between generations.

Review Questions
for Chapter 7

1. Is it possible to design a social security program that is both sound and equitable? What changes would you make in the system as it is now constituted to achieve such a goal?
2. Some people have argued that participation in social security should be voluntary. What would be the positive consequences of this change? Negative consequences?
3. Assess the factors you think influence government retirement policy now and will influence it in the future.
4. Which solution would you prefer to the problem of the declining ratio of workers to retirees? Why?

8

Retirement:
The Individual
and
the Society

It is important for students of retirement to know what retirees are like and how they live. So, in previous chapters we have reviewed data about the economic and social status of retirees, their subjective reactions to their lives in retirement, and social factors that foster or interfere with a good retirement. In addition, we have suggested that the institutionalization of retirement has important consequences for the whole society.

In this final chapter we will view retirement in a broader perspective. Because retirees are but one segment of the society, we will discuss how retirees measure up to others in the society; because retirement is a phenomenon of the later years, we will explore certain age-related aspects of retirement; and, because retirement affects and is affected by conditions in the whole society, we will consider the dynamic interplay between the retired individual and the society as a whole.

The first section of this chapter will deal with the status of retired individuals as it compares with other sectors of the population, and problems of interpreting the data on older individuals' subjective reactions to their status. In the second section, we will return to a familiar theme of the book: the relationship between the individual, the society, and social change.

Throughout this book we have emphasized that retirement is a social process. It is public laws, company rules, and informal social norms that have established retirement as the thing to do in one's later years, that specify the appropriate age to retire, and that provide economic and other support to retirees. Yet it is individuals who must make decisions about retirement and fashion lives for themselves in retirement. A good deal of the sociological literature has been concerned with these individual aspects of retirement—factors influencing decisions to retire, subjective reactions to retirement, and the quality of life for the individual who has retired.

Most of the research on the lives of retirees that we have cited has limited its focus to the picture of retirees' lives at one point in time. Recall that these studies provide important information about retirees' financial status, such as levels of social security benefits and the number of people with dual pensions at given periods. Studies we have reviewed give a rough idea about how many retired persons work part-time; what the activities, social ties, and attitudes of retired people are; and what the variations are within the retired population at a particular period. This type of information is valuable, but insufficient to assess the position of retirees. Further insights are gained by comparisons of the position of retirees with other segments of the population and by looking at retirees at several points in their life careers. Indeed, it is difficult to interpret data on retirees without such comparisons. For example, in Chapter 3 we asked just how low is the average income level of retirees. Is it nearly the same or considerably lower than that of younger persons? How does it compare with the retiree's preretirement income? We have interspersed several such comparisons in early chapters. Here we summarize and systematize comparative data on the economic, health, and marital status of retirees. The results are quite consistent; they confirm what most of us suspect. Available "objective" indicators of the status of retirees show that retirees *are* relatively disadvantaged.

The Relative Status of the Retired: A Review

We pull together material on the relative position of retirees that has been analyzed from three different perspectives: (1) viewing the stratum of retired people against the background of all adult strata in our society; (2) comparing retirees with older people who are still employed; and (3) examining the previous income and health history of individual retirees. Most of the data on which we rely here are objective in the sense that they tend to be independent of retirees' own evaluations—income and marital status, for example. Some of the measures of health, however, are based on the retiree's own assessment. We have included them since there appears to be a correlation between physicians' evaluations and those of the people themselves. Finally, it is important to note that our review focuses on retirees as a whole, rather than on variations within the retired population.

Retired versus Working-Age Adults. Consider the relative status of retirees and of adults under 60 or 65. Because employment provides the individual with an important source of social identity in our society, the social status of retirees is generally lower than that of people who are economically active. Perhaps more important, the financial status of retired people is not as good, on the average, as that of working-age people. Retired persons, who make up a large proportion of the older population, have lower incomes than working-age adults. Many retirees have incomes low enough to be considered poverty level. We know that a higher percentage of the older population as a whole than of younger adults is below the poverty line.

Although a relatively small percentage of retired persons is bedfast or housebound and most can get around outside their homes by themselves (Bond, 1976), retired people are not as healthy as younger adults. Older people in general are much more likely to be limited in their major activities than are younger adults. They are more likely to be suffering from such chronic diseases as asthma, chronic bronchitis, heart conditions, arthritis, diabetes, and hypertension; they are less likely than younger adults to have good vision and good hearing (U.S. Department of Commerce, 1977). As we have seen, a substantial proportion of retirees report limitations in their major activity.

Another disadvantage of retired persons is that more of them are widowed than are working-age adults. Among all people 65 and over, 14% of the men and 52% of the women were widowed in 1978. Proportions of widowed people among those under 65 are much lower. Even among persons 55–64, about 3% of the men and 18% of the women were widowed in 1978. As for retired people specifically, rates of widowhood are also higher than for younger adults (Lauriat & Rabin, 1976; U.S. Bureau of the Census, 1979b; see also Chapter 3).

Thus, considering several "objective" indexes of well-being, retired people and the older population as a whole are not as well off as adults under 65.

Retired versus Employed Older People. In 1977 a little more than 1 million men and women 65 and over were working year-round, full-time (U.S. Bureau of the Census, 1977). By and large these employed older people are more advantaged than their retired counterparts. As we noted in Chapter 3, differences in income between these two segments of the older population are quite marked. Not only do the retired have lower incomes than older people who are employed but the longer the period of retirement, the lower the income on the average.

Retired people as compared with older people who are still working have other disadvantages as well. In a national sample of men and women 65 and over in 1968, the employed had higher incomes than the retired, and they were somewhat younger (Jaslow, 1976; G. B. Thompson, 1973). The retirees in this sample were also less likely than the employed to assess their health as average or good. Two-thirds of the retired, compared with 81% of the employed, men assessed their health as average or good. The corresponding percentages for women are 72% and 86%.

Pre- and Postretirement. Several longitudinal studies are now available that follow the same individuals within particular cohorts from their preretirement to postretirement years. In addition, some research has included questions to retirees about their past, so we have some retrospective data.

According to these longitudinal studies, retired people do experience losses and show decrements as compared with earlier periods in their lives. For one thing, the income of retirees is substantially lower than it was before retirement. Particularly within the last few years, they have felt the pinch of inflation. Many now report that they have had to reduce their standard of living. Second, just as the health of older people as a whole deteriorates with aging, on balance the health of retirees also tends to grow worse. However, as discussed in Chapter 5, there is little evidence that deteriorating health is the result of retirement; rather, it appears to be a process that occurs with aging. In fact, some people's health seems to improve after they retire.

Subjective Reactions

Taken as a whole, these comparisons dramatize the disadvantaged position of the retired population. They are worse off than people of working age, than older people who are still employed, and than they were before retirement. Whatever reference point retirees might use to judge their present position, they generally suffer by comparison. Yet, as we have seen, on the whole retirees' feelings about retired life do not seem to mirror these relative deprivations. For more than a decade, a solid majority of retirees have evinced positive responses to retirement.

Further, if we undertake a comparative analysis of retirees' subjective reactions similar to the comparative analysis of "objective" indexes of their well-being—by comparing the relative satisfactions of retirees with other sectors of the society—the patterns of these two sets of comparisons are not the same. For example:

- *Retired versus employed men and women 65 and over.* In 1968 the morale of the retired was only slightly lower than the morale of the employed once income, age, and ability to function were controlled in the analysis (Jaslow, 1976; G. B. Thompson, 1973). Similarly, in 1971, controlling for differences in race, marital status, sex, income, health, and education, the researchers found that older people who were still working were just slightly more satisfied with their lives than those who had retired (Campbell, Converse, & Rodgers, 1976).

- *Pre- and postretirement.* As noted in Chapter 5, a 1978 national survey found that approximately two-fifths of retired people felt that the quality of retired life was somewhat or much better than life when they were working; about one-quarter said that it was the same as life when they were working (Harris, 1979).
- *Older versus working-age adults.* When samples of the entire older population are compared with samples of younger people, older people are more likely than younger people to say they are satisfied with life in general and with specific domains of life (see Chapter 5). Data on life satisfaction comparing only the retired with younger persons are not available.

In sum, retired people are generally worse off than other segments of the population in terms of income, health, and marital status; but their sense of well-being, on the whole, seems to be as positive as others' and as high as it was before retirement. How do we interpret these findings? Are such subjective reactions as paradoxical as they seem?

Variations among Retirees. The data summarized above refer to retirees in general and therefore pass over the great variations within the retired population (and the older population as a whole). Retirees' personalities and strategies for coping, of course, differ. Perhaps more important, some retirees are *not* disadvantaged. Some have good incomes, and some have more social supports than others—for example, men especially are likely to be married. Although there is a high rate of chronic ailments among the retired, most can get about and a majority assess their health as average or good. And, as noted in Chapter 5, good health and relatively high income are positively associated with retirement satisfaction. At least for some retirees, then, favorable responses to retirement reflect a comfortable life situation. In fact, while people in the more interesting, prestigious, and well-paying jobs often try to stave off retirement, once retired they seem to enjoy retired life (Bixby, 1976; Ingraham, 1974; Wikstrom, 1978).

However, even the relatively comfortable retirees experience some losses—the prestige and power of their former jobs, for example. Moreover, among the more disadvantaged members of the retired population, many individuals profess to be satisfied with retirement. We therefore look to other explanations to help account for retirees' apparent satisfaction with retired life.

Period of Study. Was there something about the social and economic conditions during the period when retirees were studied that might have influenced their responses? Many studies were carried out during periods of relative economic stability in American society. Perhaps this stability nurtured a sense of security among retirees that, in turn, contributed to favorable feelings about retirement.

Evidence that bears on this hypothesis is mixed. On the one hand, as noted in Chapter 5, studies from the relatively stable mid-1960s through the unsettling, inflationary mid-to-late 1970s show a good deal of consistency in the proportion of people expressing some type of positive reaction to retirement. However, the questions used to gauge feelings about retirement vary from study to study and explore different dimensions of satisfaction with retirement. On the other hand, one set of research using similar questions in two different periods found a decline in satisfaction with retirement over an eight-year span. In 1968 respondents were asked: "Generally speaking, have you found your life since retirement enjoyable?" In the 1976 survey the question was: "Generally speaking, how do you feel about your life since retirement?" Responses to these questions could range from very positive to very negative. Whereas 75% of the retired respondents showed favorable attitudes to retirement in 1968, by 1976 only 56% did so (Barfield & Morgan, 1978b). It is possible that the drop in satisfaction with retirement was due to high inflation rates in 1976 in contrast to the relatively stable price levels in the mid-1960s. We know that people at moderate or even higher income levels were concerned about the increased cost of essentials—food, heating their homes, transportation—to say nothing about high prices for leisure activities. However, the 1976 survey did not include questions about inflation or how inflation might affect retirees' feelings about retired life.

The nature of trends in satisfaction with retirement remains ambiguous. It is well to recall that at no time since the 1960s has a majority of retirees expressed a negative reaction to retired life.

Aging and Cohort Succession. Let us focus on the age-related processes of aging and cohort succession and how these processes might affect responses to retired life. Is there something about growing older itself that helps people accommodate losses and decrements? Is there something about the experiences of the particular cohorts of retired people studied that accounts for their feelings about retirement?

Consider the *aging process*. As individuals grow older, they experience physiological and psychological changes and undergo transformations in social roles and social status. We have noted earlier that scattered research suggests that one reaction to such changes among people reaching their sixties and seventies is to lower their expectations about what they can accomplish and what they can get out of life. One hears an older person say, with some resignation, "My memory isn't what it used to be." An avid tennis player will switch from physically tiring singles matches to less demanding games of doubles. Others will grin and bear baldness and wrinkles. Older people accept the fact that their children, having left home and having had children of their own, feel more responsibility for their own families than for their elderly parents. Goals of achievement are foresworn; even before retirement many people had to come to terms with the fact that they did not make it to the top. Aches and pains are anticipated. People face their own mortality by making wills or buying funeral plots. True, we have learned that some of the losses to which many people resign themselves are not inevitable. Physical stamina can be maintained well into the later years, if a judicious regimen of regular exercise is undertaken. Certain kinds of memories are also maintained well into the seventies. Nevertheless, as the sociologist W. I. Thomas proposed, if people define a situation as real, it is real in its consequences. Thus people's evaluations of their lives in retirement are likely to be affected by what they think are realistic goals at this stage of their lives. Generally, their goals are more modest than at earlier stages. Indeed, merely surviving to old age is often considered an accomplishment and a source of satisfaction. In short, one reason that retired people tend to be satisfied with their relatively low rewards is that they have lowered their aspirations for what the good life can be for people their age.

A second process we think occurs is that as people grow older they redefine what is rewarding. When sociologists refer to social rewards they usually mean three types of benefits: money or other material rewards; prestige, the social honor of their fellow men and women; and power, the ability to have their way, even if others are opposed. As people age, another type of reward becomes important: freedom to enjoy leisure. (Perhaps we can think of this as a type of power: not power over others, but power to do as one pleases.) A remark of a retired respondent in a 1976 survey epitomizes the relative importance of leisure versus money, for example. Respondents were asked how they felt about their lives since retirement. Said one retiree: "Enjoy every minute of it! Have the time at last to do just as I want or not do anything if I want that. Wouldn't trade for all the money in the world!" (Barfield & Morgan, 1978b, p. 20). These researchers note that most comments about the satisfaction of life after retirement—some put forward even by those in poor health—tended to concentrate on freedom from the demands of work and the ability to enjoy leisure. Retirement appears to have its own rewards.

A third process associated with aging involves stability rather than change. Evidence we have cited indicates that there is much continuity in the lives of retirees (see Chapter 3). Retirees have little control over decrements in physical functioning, reduction in income, and loss of loved ones. Where they can exercise some control over their lives, however, they continue the kinds of activities they had participated in before retirement. By and large most retirees maintain the same level of volunteer work, club membership, sports, religious attendance, cultural participation, reading, and television watching as they had before retirement. About half of them report increasing social contacts with relatives. Such continuity in the lives of retirees undoubtedly helps to offset the sharp changes they undergo as they give up the work roles of a lifetime.

In sum, certain processes associated with growing older appear to contribute to retirees' satisfaction with retired life—adjusting to losses over which they have little control by lowering their expectations and reevaluating what is rewarding and maintaining activities and relationships over which they do have some control.

The *unique cohort experiences* of today's retirees may also have influenced the way they react to retired life. Everyone must age; the way the individual ages varies not only among individuals but with the social and physical environment in which people grow up and grow older. The majority of retirees in the mid-1970s were born before World War I; a sizable number were born around the turn of the century. The world in which these people learned norms and values was quite different from the world of today. Many of today's retirees had farm and rural backgrounds. More than half the people born in 1900, for example, lived in rural areas when they were age 5–9; 37% of them were still in rural areas when they were age 25–29. This 1900 cohort had relatively little formal education. A quarter of the cohort had less than eight grades of schooling; another 45% had between eight and eleven years of formal education. Thus, few were graduated from high school or went to college. Many members of this cohort had early experiences with death. Almost one-quarter had one parent who died before they themselves were age 15 (see Table 8-1).

Is there something about such experiences that might affect the later attitudes of members of the cohort and the way they fit into the retirement

TABLE 8-1. *Demographic Perspectives on Three Cohorts*

	Cohort of		
Cohort Characteristics	1870 %	1900 %	1930 %
Select childhood characteristics			
Rural when age 5–9	78	59	51
Distribution by number of siblings			
0–1	6	14	29
2–3	14	25	34
4+	80	61	37
With parent who died before child reached age 15	27	22	11
Distribution by number of school years completed			
less than 8	44	28	8
8–H.S. 3	42	45	25
H.S. 4+	14	27	67
Select adult characteristics			
Rural when age 25–29	47	37	28
Distribution of males by occupation when age 35–39			
white collar	NA	31	44
blue collar	NA	52	53
farm	NA	17	3

Adapted from "Demographic Change and Problems of the Aged," by P. Uhlenberg. In *Aging from Birth to Death*, by M. W. Riley (Ed.). Copyright 1979 by the American Association for the Advancement of Science. Reprinted by permission.

role? Perhaps the social environment of people growing up before World War I—being brought up on farms, where economic livelihood depended a good deal on the vagaries of the weather and the market; being all too familiar with death at all life stages; being shut off from an awareness of alternatives because of their limited education—encouraged acceptance of whatever life had to offer. Retirees holding such values today might well define many of their ills and losses as inevitable, as God's will, and be satisfied with what they feel cannot be changed.

Unfortunately, we cannot test these ideas, since data on the values of successive cohorts of retirees are not available. But there are possible ramifications to the different social contexts in which oncoming cohorts of retirees have matured. Some retirees of the next century came to maturity in a social environment characterized by distrust of social institutions and skepticism about political leaders. Those who will retire in the year 2015 or so were the "me" generation of the 1970s. With such a background and with higher levels of education than today's retirees, will future cohorts of retirees accept losses associated with retirement as inevitable?

Retirement, the Individual, and Age-Related Processes

As we have seen, retirees generally seem favorably disposed to retirement, despite their relative disadvantages. We suggest that complex age-related processes help account for this disjunction between "objective" conditions and subjective responses. Limited evidence indicates that the aging process is accompanied not only by reductions in material and physical status in our society, but also by various psychological adjustments to these declines: people expect losses and cope accordingly. But such longitudinal evidence as we have on these matters is typically limited to one cohort of retirees and covers no more than a decade or so of the individual's life course. It is possible that not only changes with aging account for retirees' feelings but also the unique life histories of the current cohorts of retirees. Perhaps, because of their unique life histories, current cohorts of retirees have been disposed to accept disappointments throughout their lives. Even some of the objective conditions are a result of the unique experiences with which today's retirees grew up and matured. How many of the health problems of retirees today can be attributed to earlier exposure to poor nutrition, poor sanitation, harmful medications, and unsafe work environments, the dangers of which we have only recently become aware?

We have no data to shed light on the impact of both aging processes and cohort experiences in influencing today's cohorts of retirees. Social scientists have only recently understood the need to collect longitudinal data on successive cohorts of retirees. (See, for example, Riley, 1973; Riley, Johnson, & Foner, 1972.) We can be sure that new generations of retirees will be different from the people who are now retired because the society and the environment are continually changing.

Retirement and the Society: Dilemmas and Solutions

Social and economic changes not only will alter the face of retirement in the future but will also pose new problems for the retired individual and the society. The rapid pace of social change in modern societies and the dilemmas accompanying these changes should not, however, obscure the nature of these dilemmas. Retirement as a mass phenomenon has occurred primarily in the modern era in industrial societies, but the problem that institutionalized retirement addresses is universal: dealing with social replacement. Rapid social change merely highlights the problem.

Retirement: One Solution to a Universal Problem

In all societies there is a continuous flow of new cohorts into the social system while old cohorts die out. Societies must somehow construct a method for managing this succession of cohorts. Room must be made for young people who are on the threshold of adulthood and for adults already in their prime years who expect promotions to positions of leadership and authority. The problem for the society is how to get people into and out of the valued roles that are available with a minimum of social disturbance.

One solution is to allow nature to take its course. That is, older people give up their roles when they feel ready to do so or when they become ill or die so that others can step into these roles. This method characterizes earlier periods in the history of the United States. A "voluntary" system was possible because of relatively high mortality rates and a shortage of workers which, by and large, guaranteed there would be openings for the young as well as those older people who survived. The fact that many workers were in agriculture facilitated such a solution. Farmers frequently were able to taper off their activities so that their exit from work roles was not precipitous; all the while younger adults would assume greater and greater responsibility.

Another solution is to regulate the continuous flow of people in and out of roles by establishing firm age norms for entering roles and leaving them—for example, requiring children to enter school at age 6 and remain in school until age 16, or specifying a minimum age of eligibility for elective office. Retirement is a special case of this general practice; it sets age limits for remaining in the work force. In the United States, retirement has been the usual (and sometimes mandatory) arrangement for people 65 and over for less than 50 years. As the number and proportion of older people in our society grew, accommodating both new and old cohorts of workers in the work force became increasingly problematic. A major impetus to the institutionalization of retirement, however, was the Great Depression which, in turn, was a factor in the creation of the social security system. This, in effect, defined age 65 as the appropriate age for leaving the labor force.

Whether social replacement is left to "natural" forces or regulated by firm age norms for entering and leaving social roles, there are likely to be inherent problems for the society and the individual in these procedures. Consider the potential difficulties in "voluntary" arrangements. At first glance, letting nature take its course seems to be a fair system that would ensure smooth transitions of younger people into and older people out of social roles. However, there is no guarantee that the readiness of the older people to give up their valued roles will mesh with the readiness of those who are waiting to assume these roles. Instead of a smooth process of succession, there are frequently age conflicts between the "ins" and the "outs." (See, for example, Fischer, 1978 for instances of such age conflicts in early America.) Youth kept in a prolonged period of dependency and subordination sometimes resort to deviant behavior. Such problems are found in societies very different from our own as well; studies of preindustrial, undifferentiated, and preliterate societies indicate that social conflicts over the timing of transitions of young people to adult roles are pervasive. (For a fuller discussion of problems of life course transitions, see Foner & Kertzer, 1979.)

Strict rules of transition that set definite ages for entering or leaving roles eliminate uncertainty, thus permitting individuals and organizations to plan ahead. Since these rules apply to everyone alike, they appear to be democratic and equitable; but, because firm age norms cover everyone, individual variation in ability and needs are not taken into consideration. In the case of retirement, some people want to and are capable of continuing to work well beyond the usual age of retirement. Their exclusion from the labor force constitutes a loss to both the society and the individuals involved.

Currently such dilemmas are expressed in debates around three different proposals for dealing with retirement: (1) mandatory retirement, (2) raising the age at which people can become eligible for retirement benefits, and (3) introducing flexible retirement to allow those who wish to retire at the normal retirement age or earlier to do so and permit others to remain working.

Mandatory retirement at specified ages clearly has advantages. It permits both employees and employers to plan ahead. For the employer, it provides a way of moving unproductive older workers out of the work force and making room for the advancement of younger workers. It avoids the problem of having to decide age of retirement on an individual basis and of devising appropriate tests of competence. Such a procedure is not only inefficient from the employer's point of view but can also be distressing to workers. Retiring because of prescribed rules may be less psychologically painful than having one's performance judged inadequate.

The disadvantages are similar to those associated with strict age norms. The rights of those who are physically and mentally capable of working and who want to continue working are ignored. Their withdrawal from the labor force constitutes a loss of productivity to the whole society. Further, to the extent that mandatory retirement adds to the number of retirees in the society, it increases financial costs to the society.

For the time being, the debate about mandatory retirement has been partially resolved by legislation extending the permissible mandatory retirement age from 65 to 70 for most enterprises. What effect raising the age limit for mandatory retirement will have is unclear. Even before the permissible age of mandatory retirement was raised, many jobs were not subject to mandatory retirement rules. According to one analysis of new beneficiaries in 1968, a considerable number of workers who were covered by mandatory retirement rules retired before the age specified by the firm. And among those who did retire at the mandatory age, many were willing to retire (Schulz, 1974). See Figure 8-1, which illustrates various retirement patterns among a cohort of male workers who retired in 1968. The National Longitudinal Survey showed similar findings. Only 3% of the more than 2000 retirements that occurred among their sample of men over the decade 1966–1976 could realistically be classified as mandatory, that is, removal from jobs by the operation of mandatory retirement plans (Parnes, 1979).

Recent estimates by economists also suggest that relatively few additional workers will remain in the labor force as a result of the new legislation. In 1977 hearings before the Senate Subcommittee on Labor, expert witnesses estimated that these additional older workers would raise the overall rate of labor force participation by less than 1% (Rhine, 1978). Still, there are some signs that more older workers will elect to stay in the labor force than this analysis suggests. In interviews with executives of several large corporations, spot reports indicate that quite a few workers are staying on the job past age 65. To cite one example, Sears, Roebuck and Co. reported that 77% of the salaried and 61% of the hourly employees scheduled to retire in 1978 had elected to stay past age 65 (Hayes, 1979).

It is too early to tell what the eventual impact of raising the permissible mandatory retirement age will be. If current overall patterns of age at retirement are maintained—that is, if relatively few older workers elect to remain in the labor force beyond age 65—then another proposal, a modified flexible retirement, would in effect be operating. A truly flexible retirement policy—with the complete elimination of mandatory retirement—has been established for the federal government and in a few states. There is, as yet, no legislation barring mandatory retirement in the nation as a whole.

Perhaps a third proposal, raising the age of entitlement to full pension benefits beyond age 65, will become a pressing issue. As noted in Chapter 7, such a policy would discourage early retirement, thus violating what many workers had come to expect as their right. It might also retard the promotion

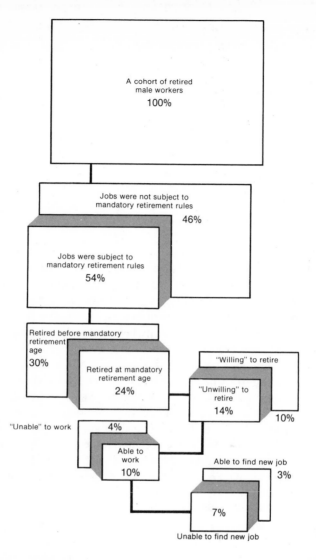

FIGURE 8-1. The Incidence of Mandatory Retirement. (From "The Economics of Mandatory Retirement," by J. Schulz. In Aging and Work, 1974, 1 (Winter), 5. Copyright 1974 by the National Council on the Aging, Inc. Reprinted by permission.)

of younger workers. Advancing the age of normal retirement has one advantage: as with mandatory retirement, it would permit planning ahead.

In sum, all proposals dealing with the issue of retirement age have both advantages and disadvantages. We cannot predict what specific proposals will be adopted, but changes in retirement policies are bound to come. The inevitability of change points to still another dilemma—the possible gap between public policy and individual expectations.

The Succession of Cohorts and Dilemmas of Retirement

Current debates about retirement policy are a reflection of demographic, economic, and social change. We now understand, in a way that perhaps the framers of early retirement policies in our country did not, that retirement programs will be continually subject to alterations. We also understand now that, while new policies can often resolve some immediate difficulties, these innovations may also produce unintended consequences.

Retirees—Yesterday, Today, and Tomorrow. Consider the early cohorts of retirees. From the point of view of the policymakers, retirement helped to ease older workers out of the labor force at a time of labor surplus. Policymakers saw the social security program as providing a floor of economic support to retirees and a dignified way of moving older people out of the work force. But, as welcome as social security benefits surely were to the retirees of the 1940s and early 1950s, retirement was a new role to them. There were no guidelines about what the appropriate behavior and activities for retirees should be; they had to shape the retirement role on their own. For the most part, this was an individual matter, since the number of retirees at that time was relatively small and there was no network for bringing retirees together. Further, there was little in their background to pave the way for what was essentially a leisure role. Not their education: retirees born in the latter part of the 19th century had even lower levels of education than the 1900 cohort (see Table 8-1 again). Not their values: these retirees were brought up to honor hard work and achievement. Thus, early cohorts of retirees had to deal with a role for which they were ill-prepared.

Today's retirees have had the advantage of entering an established role and learning from the forerunners—even if only learning what not to do. Retirees today benefit from an array of economic and social supports provided by communities and the national government. They have come to expect retirement as a right, and many look forward to retirement. The rub is that their enjoyment of retired life is now being slowly eroded by nationwide problems like inflation and the energy crisis, problems that they did not—could not—foresee.

The full irony of the situation will be faced by tomorrow's retirees and potential retirees. They have been brought up in an era when retirement has come to be accepted as a right; they have many personal resources to make their lives as retirees interesting and meaningful. Compared with earlier cohorts, they will be better educated; more will have been in high-level, white-collar jobs where they have had opportunities to exercise independent judgment. If the association between health and education continues, they will be healthier than earlier cohorts. More than previous cohorts, these future cohorts seem prepared to make retirement an enriching experience. Yet it is precisely these new cohorts who face a change in the rules of the game. Whether it is the elimination of mandatory retirement, the introduction of fully flexible retirement policies, or the pushing up of normal retirement age beyond 65, new cohorts will be asked to adjust to changes they had not expected. If the energy crisis persists, we can only speculate about how cohorts who expect personal frontiers to continually expand and who cherish freedom of movement will adjust to curtailment and limitations of opportunities.

We see, then, that each new cohort of retirees has had to face and will face new social and economic conditions for which its members are not prepared. It is an article of faith in our society that people must plan ahead. When retirees are asked to give advice to younger people about retirement, the retirees emphasize the need for planning early (Harris, 1979). Without minimizing the importance of future planning, let us recognize the obstacles confronting individuals who want to plan ahead for a retirement in an uncertain future.

Will social institutions be any better prepared to accommodate the new types of retirees of the future? To a certain extent some social institutions are already gearing up for increasing numbers of older people who want to make their leisure time a period of continued personal growth. Colleges and universities are expanding programs of continuing education to attract older students, for example. Legislators have devised a social security schedule that takes population trends into consideration and aims to ensure the viability of the social security system in the future.

But lower fertility rates today mean not only a reduced worker-to-retiree ratio in the next century; they also portend fewer children per retiree, the consequence being that many retirees will not be able to depend on children in times of need.

Two other trends will also affect the availability of social supports for retired people. First, rising divorce rates mean that more retirees will enter the retirement period without a spouse. Second, the ratio of males to females in the older age categories is already low. Given the likelihood that male mortality rates will continue to be higher than female mortality rates among those 65 and over, many older women will be widowed.[1] Thus, whether because of divorce or widowhood, many retired people—particularly women— will not have a spouse to rely on. In short, future cohorts of retirees may be even less likely than the retired cohorts of today to be able to count on the emotional support and services of children and spouse. Few signs are available

---

[1] As many behavioral differences between men and women are reduced—for example, increased cigarette smoking among women—female mortality rates may increase and thus the gap between male and female mortality rates among those 65 and over may decline.

---

to indicate whether social institutions in the future will be prepared to meet the needs of unmarried and childless retirees.

In addition to future needs of retirees that we can foresee, social institutions will have to deal with developments that we cannot predict. We cannot, for example, predict how retirees will respond if their expectations are not met. One possibility is that retirees who have exercised initiative or who have had administrative experience in their former jobs will organize self-help groups. Another possibility, especially among retirees who have experienced political dissent, is organized political action. These initiatives could lead to unanticipated trends, which brings us to our final point: retirees are not merely passive adjusters to existing conditions. In fact, their actions are frequently the impetus for social institutions to move (see Riley, 1978).

Interaction between Individual and Society

The retirement process involves an interplay between the individual and the society. Social developments—like changing economic conditions, changing roles of men and women, urbanization, and energy crises—impinge on the individual. It is the individual who must cope with the loss of a job or high prices, changing neighborhoods, life without a spouse, curtailed travel, or a poorly heated or poorly cooled home. In turn, as people cope with and react to these societal changes, their responses will affect the whole society, setting into motion new processes of change.

Think of the unanticipated increase in early retirement. Legislation permitting retirees to retire between ages 62 and 65 with reduced benefits certainly encouraged early retirement. But it was thousands of individuals making decisions on their own to retire early with reduced retirement benefits rather than continue to work that added up to a ground swell. In turn, these thousands of early retirees had an impact on the social security system. By reducing revenues to the system and increasing the load of retirees to be supported, the trend toward early retirement served to aggravate the system's financial problems. Now, as a result of these problems, new programs are being introduced. These programs meet short-term needs of the social security system, but higher taxes, altered replacement ratios, and other provisions of the new legislation run counter to the needs of many individuals. We have yet to see the ripple effects of these new policies.

In short, individual and societal agendas often do not mesh. Individuals and social institutions both respond to social changes affecting retirement; but individuals cope with these changes with the resources at hand, including the habits and values of a lifetime. In fashioning responses to social change, individuals leave their mark on the society. On their part, social agencies often do not immediately address salient social issues; typically the development of social programs lags behind pressing social needs.

In addition, when these programs *are* implemented, they frequently have unintended consequences that generate new problems. Thus, as societies change, problems associated with retirement will continually crop up. If we understand that such problems are inevitable and that there are no permanent solutions to them, we will be more alert to potential difficulties in retirement policies, we will understand the need for constant monitoring of societal trends and individual reactions to these trends, and we will recognize the importance of policy decisions being made with both short-run needs and long-term trends in mind.

Review Questions
for Chapter 8

1. *In light of the disadvantages experienced by retired people, how can retirees' positive reactions to retirement be explained?*
2. *Suppose that mandatory retirement were completely eliminated in the United States. What might some of the economic, social, and political consequences be?*
3. *Think ahead to the time when you will be of retirement age. What kind of plans do you think you can make for this period in your life? What problems do you foresee in making such plans? Do you think that societal agencies can plan ahead for 20 and 30 years?*

Glossary

aged dependency ratio: Number of people aged 65 and over divided by number of people of working age (20–64). It provides an estimate of the number of old persons to be supported by working-age persons.

Age Discrimination in Employment Act: Forbids discrimination against workers under age 70 on the basis of age, with a few exceptions.

agism: Prejudice or discrimination (usually against older people) on the basis of age.

anticipatory socialization: The process of learning the behaviors and attitudes associated with a role before the individual is actually in the role.

benefit base: The maximum amount of wages that can be credited to a worker's social security record for a given calendar year. This is the portion of earnings subject to payroll taxes. In 1980, the benefit base was $25,900.

birthrate: Number of births per thousand women per year.

cohort: The aggregate of individuals born in the same time interval.

cohort differences: Variations in size or composition of different cohorts and in the particular segment of history to which each cohort has been exposed.

cross-sectional comparisons: Comparisons based on questioning or observation of two or more categories of persons—for example, older people and younger people—at one point in time.

death benefit: A lump-sum death benefit may be made on the social security record of a worker who dies while insured under the program. The payment may be no more than $255.

downward mobility: Movement of an individual in a social hierarchy that is accompanied by a reduction in social rewards.

early retirement: Retirement before age 65.

earnings test: The social security law provides that a beneficiary who has substantial earnings from work will have some or all cash benefits withheld, depending on the amount of annual earnings. Insured workers (and their dependents or survivors) may draw benefits regardless of earnings when they reach age 72.

Employee Retirement Income Security Act: Requires private pension plans to guarantee minimum vesting rights for employer contributions.

fertility rate: The rate of reproduction.

general revenue taxes: Government revenue that is not collected for the funding of a particular program.

labor force: The aggregate of people working or unemployed—that is, not working but looking for work.

life-course transitions: Points in the life course when the individual relinquishes one set of roles and assumes new ones.

longitudinal studies: observation (or questioning) of the same individuals over a period of time.

mandatory retirement: A policy requiring workers to retire by a certain age. Recent federal policy forbids mandatory retirement before age 70 in most instances.

median income: The income amount that divides the distribution of incomes in half. That is, half the population has an income above and half the population has an income below the median-income level.

OASDHI (Old Age, Survivor, Disability and Health Insurance): The program that administers benefits to people, their survivors and dependents, who qualify under the old-age (retirement), survivors, disability, and health insurance provisions of the Social Security Act.

pay-as-you-go tax and benefit scheme: Program whose benefits are financed by recently collected taxes.

poverty level: The amounts of income below which families of different size and composition cannot purchase nutritionally adequate diets. The food budget used as the basis of an adequate diet is the Department of Agriculture's economy food plan for emergency use or for use when funds are very low.

Primary Insurance Amount: The amount that would be payable to a worker who retires and draws benefits from social security at age 65. This amount, which is related to the worker's average monthly earnings, is also used as the basis of computation for all types of benefits paid to secondary beneficiaries, such as wife, widow, or children.

reduced social security benefits: Retired-worker benefits first received at ages 62–64 are permanently reduced by 5/9 of 1% (maximum reduction of 20%) for each month before age 65.

regressive taxes: Taxes that fall more heavily on lower- than higher-income people.

replacement rate: The extent to which income received in retirement replaces preretirement income.

retired-worker benefits: Social security payments made to individuals who retire (earn less than a specified amount), are at least age 62, and have worked a sufficient length of time in jobs covered by social security.

retirement: Definitions vary, but generally defined as reduction of or withdrawal from participation in the labor force in later stages of life, or as the receipt of social security or other pension income.

role: The pattern of specific rights and duties associated with the parts people play in society.

role discontinuities: Sharp changes in the types of roles the individual fills and in what is expected of the person.

role model: A person whose attitudes and behavior in a particular role provide a standard that another individual follows in performing the same role.

social rewards: Benefits individuals receive for performance in a role. These typically take the form of money or other material goods, prestige, and power.

social security: The Social Security Act of 1935 and related laws established a number of programs that provide financial and/or medical assistance to various groups of people. The programs include retirement insurance, survivor's insurance, disability income, hospital and medical insurance for the aged and disabled, black-lung benefits, supplemental security income, unemployment insurance, and public assistance and welfare services. Unemployment insurance and public assistance and welfare services are operated by the states with federal cooperation; the other programs are directly operated by the federal government.

social security payroll tax: OASDHI programs are financed by taxes on earnings. In 1980, employers and employees each contributed at the rate of 6.13% of the first $25,900 of the employee's earnings.

social security trust fund: Amounts equivalent to the social security contributions are deposited in trust funds from which social security benefits are paid. Funds not needed for current benefits and administrative expenses are invested in interest-bearing federal securities.

social support: Social support takes many forms: helping and encouraging, offering comfort and affection, or affirming an individual's worth.

socioeconomic status: The ranking of an individual in a social hierarchy based on the unequal distribution of money, power, and prestige.

SSI (Supplementary Security Income): The first federally administered cash-assistance program in this country available to the general public. It is designed to provide a floor of income to the aged, blind, or disabled person who has little or no income and resources.

student beneficiary program: A full-time student is entitled to insurance benefits on the social security record of a parent if the student is 18–21 years of age and the parent is entitled to disability insurance benefits, retirement insurance benefits, or has died and was either fully or currently insured at the time of death.

survivor benefits: When a worker insured under social security dies, cash benefits may be paid to eligible survivors.

total dependency ratio: Number of people under age 20 plus the number of people 65 and over, divided by the number of people of working age, 20–64. It provides an estimate of the number of people to be supported by those of working age.

vesting: Nonforfeitable right to accrued pension benefits given workers even if they stop work before retirement age.

wife's benefits: Basically, a wife is entitled to wife's insurance benefits on her husband's social security record if he is entitled to retirement or disability insurance benefits and she is either age 62 or over, or is caring for a child under 18 years of age (or an older disabled child).

worker-to-retiree ratio: The relative number of working-age people (20–64) to the number of people 65 and over.

References

Achenbaum, W. A. *Old age in the new land*. Baltimore: Johns Hopkins University Press, 1978.

Andrisani, P. J. Effects of health problems on the work experience of middle-aged men. *Industrial Gerontology*, 1977, *4*, 97–112.

Andrisani, P. J., Appelbaum, E., Koppel, R., & Miljus, R. C. *Work attitudes and labor market experience: Evidence from the national longitudinal surveys*. Philadelphia: Center for Labor and Human Resource Studies, 1977.

Andrisani, P., & Parnes, H. S. *Five years in the work lives of middle-aged men: Findings from the national longitudinal surveys*. Paper presented at the Aspen Institute for Humanistic Studies, Aspen, August 1977.

Ash, P. Pre-retirement counseling. *The Gerontologist*, 1966, *6*, 97–99; 127.

Atchley, R. C. *The sociology of retirement*. New York: Halsted/Wiley, 1976.

Baltes, P. B., Reese, H. W., & Lipsitt, L. P. Life-span developmental psychology. *Annual Review of Psychology*, 1980, *31*, 65–110.

Baltes, P. B., & Schaie, K. W. Aging and IQ: The myth of the twilight years. *Psychology Today*, 1974, *7*, 35–40.

Baltes, P. B., & Willis, S. L. Life-span developmental psychology, cognitive functioning and social policy. In M. W. Riley (Ed.), *Aging from birth to death*. Boulder, Col.: Westview Press, 1979.

Barfield, R. E., & Morgan, J. N. *Early retirement: The decision and the experience and a second look*. Ann Arbor: The University of Michigan, Institute for Social Research, Survey Research Center, 1970.

Barfield, R. E., & Morgan, J. N. Trends in planned early retirement. *The Gerontologist*, 1978, *18*, 13–18. (a).

Barfield, R. E., & Morgan, J. N. Trends in satisfaction with retirement. *The Gerontologist*, 1978, *18*, 19–23. (b)

Barton, E. M., Plemons, J. K., Willis, S. L., & Baltes, P. B. Recent findings on adult and gerontological intelligence: Changing a stereotype of decline. *American Behavioral Scientist*, 1975, *19*, 224–236.

Bell, B. D. Role set orientations and life satisfaction: A new look at an old theory. In J. E. Gubrium (Ed.), *Time, roles, and self in old age*. New York: Human Sciences Press, 1976.

Bengtson, V. L. Differences between subsamples in level of present role activity. In R. J. Havighurst, J. M. A. Munnichs, B. Neugarten, & H. Thomae (Eds.), *Adjustment to retirement*. Assen, The Netherlands: Van Gorcum, 1969.

Bennetts, L. When homemaking becomes job no. 2. *The New York Times*, July 14, 1979, p. 8.

Bixby, L. Retirement patterns in the United States: Research and policy interaction. *Social Security Bulletin*, 1976, *39*, 3–19.

Board of Trustees. *1980 annual report of the board of trustees of the federal old-age and survivors insurance and disability insurance trust funds*. Washington, D.C.: U.S. Government Printing Office, 1980.

Bond, K. Retirement history study's first four years: Work, health, and living arrangements. *Social Security Bulletin*, 1976, *39*, 1–13.

Booth, A. Sex and social participation. *American Sociological Review*, 1972, *37*, 183–192.

Botwinick, J. *Aging and behavior*. New York: Springer, 1973.

Botwinick, J. Intellectual abilities. In J. E. Birren & K. W. Schaie (Eds.), *Handbook of the psychology of aging*. New York: Van Nostrand Reinhold, 1977.

Bull, C. N., & Aucoin, J. B. Voluntary association participation and life satisfaction: A replication note. *Journal of Gerontology*, 1975, *30*, 73–76.

Butler, R. *Why survive? Being old in America*. New York: Harper & Row, 1975.

Campbell, A., Converse, P. E., & Rodgers, W. L. *The quality of American life*. New York: Russell Sage, 1976.

Canadian Department of Labor, Economics and Research. *Age and performance in retail trade*. Ottawa: The Queen's Printer and Controller of Stationery, 1959.

Carp, F. M. Housing and living environment of older people. In R. H. Binstock, E. Shanas, & Associates (Eds.). *Handbook of aging and the social sciences*. New York: Van Nostrand Reinhold, 1976.

Chatfield, W. Economic and sociological factors influencing life satisfaction of the aged. *Journal of Gerontology*, 1977, *32*, 593–99.

Chen, Y., & Chu, K. Future funding of social security and the total dependency ratio. *Monthly Labor Review*, 1977, *100*, 53–55.

Clement, J. Longitudinal and cross-sectional assessments of age changes in physical strength as related to sex, social class, and mental ability. *Journal of Gerontology*, 1974, *29*, 423–429.

Cobb, S. Social support and health through the life course. In M. W. Riley (Ed.), *Aging from birth to death*. Boulder, Col.: Westview Press, 1979.

Cole, S. Age and scientific performance. *American Journal of Sociology*, 1979, *84*, 958–977.

Cumming, E., & Henry, W. E. *Growing old: The process of disengagement*. New York: Basic Books, 1961.

Cutler, S. J. Voluntary association participation and life satisfaction: A cautionary research note. *Journal of Gerontology*, 1973, *28*, 96–100.

Dennis, W. Creative productivity between the ages of 20 and 80 years. *Journal of Gerontology*, 1966, *21*, 1–8.

Dowd, J., & LaRossa, R. *Primary group contact and elderly morale: An exchange/power analysis*. Unpublished paper, 1978.

Durkheim, E. *Suicide*. New York: Free Press, 1951.

Fischer, D. H. *Growing old in America* (Expanded ed.). New York: Oxford University Press, 1978.

Fisher, P. The social security crisis: An international dilemma. *Aging and Work*, 1978, *1*, 1–14.

Foner, A. *The middle years: Prelude to retirement?* Unpublished doctoral dissertation, New York University, 1969.

Foner, A. Age stratification and the changing family. In J. Demos & S. S. Boocock (Eds.), *Turning points: Historical and sociological essays on the family*. Chicago: University of Chicago Press, 1978.

Foner, A. Ascribed and achieved bases of stratification. *Annual Review of Sociology*, 1979, *5*, 219–242.

Foner, A., & Kertzer, D. I. Intrinsic and extrinsic sources of change in life-course transitions. In M. W. Riley (Ed.), *Aging from birth to death*. Boulder, Col.: Westview Press, 1979.

Fox, A. Work status and income change, 1968–72: Retirement History Study preview. *Social Security Bulletin*, 1976, *39*, 14–30.

Fox, A. Earnings replacement rates of retired couples: Findings from the Retirement History Study. *Social Security Bulletin*, 1979, *42*, 17–39.

Fox, J. H. Effects of retirement and former work life on women's adaptation in old age. *Journal of Gerontology*, 1977, *32*, 196–202.

Friedmann, E. A., & Orbach, H. L. Adjustment to retirement. *American handbook of psychiatry* (2nd ed.), 1974, *1*, 609–645.

Fromm, E. *Escape from freedom*. New York: Avon, 1965.

Gibson, R. M., & Fisher, C. R. Age differences in health care spending, fiscal year 1977. *Social Security Bulletin*, 1979, *42*, 3–16.

Gilmore, A. J. J. Community surveys and mental health. In W. F. Anderson & T. G. Judge (Eds.), *Geriatric medicine*. New York: Academic Press, 1974.

Glamser, F. D. Determinants of a positive attitude toward retirement. *Journal of Gerontology,* 1976, *31,* 104–107.

Glamser, F. D., & DeJong, G. F. The efficacy of pre-retirement preparation programs for industrial workers. *Journal of Gerontology,* 1975, *30,* 595–600.

Glick, R. Working: Who needs it? *Perspective on Aging,* 1977, *6,* 10–11.

Goody, J. Aging in non-industrial societies. In R. H. Binstock, E. Shanas, & Associates (Eds.), *Handbook of aging and the social sciences.* New York: Van Nostrand Reinhold, 1976.

Grad, S., & Foster, K. *Income of the population 55 and older, 1976.* U.S. Department of Health, Education and Welfare, Social Security Administration, Office of Policy/Office of Research and Statistics (Staff Paper No. 35). Washington, D.C.: 1979.

Harris, L., & Associates. *The myth and reality of aging in America.* Washington, D.C.: National Council on the Aging, 1975.

Harris, L., & Associates. *1979 study of American attitudes toward pensions and retirement: A nationwide survey of employees, retirees and business leaders.* New York: Johnson & Higgins, 1979.

Hayes, T. C. Gold watch: Now or later? *The New York Times,* July 11, 1979, D1; 5.

Heidbreder, E. M. Factors in retirement adjustment: White collar/blue collar experience. *Industrial Gerontology,* 1972, No. 12, 69–82.

Hess, B. B., & Waring, J. M. Parent and child in later life: Rethinking the relationship. In R. M. Lerner & G. B. Spanier (Eds.), *Child influences on marital and family interaction.* New York: Academic Press, 1978.

Hollister, R. Social mythology and reform: Income maintenance for the aged. *The Annals of the American Academy of Political and Social Science,* 1974, *415,* 19–40.

Holtzman, A. Analysis of old age politics in the United States. *Journal of Gerontology,* 1954, *9,* 56–67.

Hudson, R. B., & Binstock, R. H. Political systems and aging. In R. H. Binstock, E. Shanas, & Associates (Eds.), *Handbook of aging and the social sciences.* New York: Van Nostrand Reinhold, 1976.

Ingraham, M. H. *My purpose holds: Reactions and experiences in retirement of TIAA–CREF annuitants.* New York: Educational Research Division, TIAA–CREF, 1974.

International Labour Office. *Older workers: Work and retirement.* Report VI (1). Geneva, 1978.

Irelan, L. M., & Bell, D. B. Understanding subjectively defined retirement: A pilot analysis. *The Gerontologist,* 1972, *12,* 354–356.

Irelan, L. M., Motley, D. K., Schwab, K., Sherman, Sally R., & Murray, J. *Almost 65: baseline data from the retirement history study.* U.S. Department of Health, Education and Welfare, Social Security Administration, Office of Research and Statistics. Washington, D.C.: U.S. Government Printing Office, 1976.

Jaffe, A. J. The retirement dilemma. *Industrial Gerontology,* 1972, *14,* 1–88.

Jahoda, M., Lazarsfeld, P., & Zeisel, H. *Die Arbeitslosen von Marienthal.* Leipzig: Hirzel, 1933

Jarvik, L. F. Thoughts on the psychology of aging. *American Psychologist,* 1975, *30,* 576–583.

Jaslow, P. Employment, retirement, and morale among older women. *Journal of Gerontology,* 1976, *31,* 212–218.

Kahn, R. L. Aging and social support. In M. W. Riley (Ed.), *Aging from birth to death.* Boulder, Col.: Westview Press, 1979.

Kasschau, P. L. Reevaluating the need for retirement preparation programs. *Industrial Gerontology,* 1974, *1,* 42–59.

Kerckhoff, A. C. Family patterns and morale in retirement. In I. H. Simpson & J. C. McKinney (Eds.), *Social aspects of aging.* Durham, N.C.: Duke University Press, 1966.

Kimmel, D. C., Price, K. F., & Walker, J. W. Retirement choice and retirement satisfaction. *Journal of Gerontology,* 1978, *33,* 575–585.

Kreps, J. M. Social security in the coming decade: Questions for a mature system. *Social Security Bulletin,* 1976, *39,* 21–29.

Kuypers, J. A., & Bengtson, V. L. Social breakdown and competence. *Human Development,* 1973, *16,* 181–201.

Larson, R. Thirty years of research on the subjective well-being of older Americans. *Journal of Gerontology,* 1978, *33,* 109–125.

Lauriat, P., & Rabin, W. Characteristics of new beneficiaries by age at entitlement. In *Reaching retirement age: Findings from a survey of newly entitled workers, 1968–70.* U.S. Department of Health, Education and Welfare, Social Security Administration, Office of Research and Statistics (Research Report No. 47). Washington, D.C.: U.S. Government Printing Office, 1976.

Lemon, B. W., Bengtson, V. L., & Peterson, J. A. An exploration of the activity theory of aging: Activity types and life satisfaction among in-movers to a retirement community. *Journal of Gerontology,* 1972, *27,* 511–523.

Liem, R., & Liem, J. Social class and mental illness reconsidered: The role of economic stress and social support. *Journal of Health and Social Behavior,* 1978, *19,* 139–156.

Lowenthal, M. F., & Haven, C. Interaction and adaptation: intimacy as a critical variable. *American Sociological Review,* 1968, *33,* 20–30.

Madden, R. L. Retirees help to defeat school budgets. *The New York Times,* June 11, 1979, B–7.

Mallan, L. B., & Cox, D. Older workers uninsured for retired-worker benefits. *Social Security Bulletin,* 1978, *41,* 3–11.

Manney, J. D., Jr. *Aging in American society: An examination of concepts and issues.* Ann Arbor: University of Michigan, Wayne State University, Institute of Gerontology, 1975.

Mark, J. A. Comparative job performance by age. *Monthly Labor Review,* 1957, *80,* 1467–1471.

Merriam, I. C. Social security and social welfare indicators. *The Annals of the American Academy of Political and Social Science,* 1978, *435,* 117–139.

Merton, R. K. *Social theory and social structure.* New York: Free Press, 1957.

Miller, S. J. The social dilemma of the aging leisure participant. In A. M. Rose & W. A. Peterson (Eds.), *Older people and their social worlds.* Philadelphia: Davis, 1965.

Mincer, J. Labor force participation. *International encyclopedia of the social sciences* (Vol. 8). New York: Macmillan, 1968, 474–481.

Motley, D. K. Availability of retired persons for work: Findings from the retirement history study. *Social Security Bulletin,* 1978, *41,* 1–12.

O'Meara, J. R. *Retirement: Reward or rejection?* New York: The Conference Board, 1977.

Ostfeld, A. M. The aging brain: Alzheimer's disease and senile dementia—Discussant's perspective. In A. M. Ostfeld & D. C. Gibson (Eds.), *Epidemiology of aging.* U.S. Department of Health, Education and Welfare. Washington, D.C.: U.S. Government Printing Office, 1972.

Parnes, H. S. Summary and conclusions. In H. S. Parnes, G. Nestel, T. N. Chirikos, T. N. Daymont, F. L. Mott, D. O. Parsons, & Associates, *From the middle to the later years: Longitudinal studies of the preretirement and postretirement experiences of men* (Vol. 5 in *The Preretirement Years* series). Columbus: Ohio State University, Center for Human Resources, 1979.

Parnes, H. S., Adams, A. V., Andrisani, P. J., Kohen, A., & Nestel, G. *The pre-retirement years: Four years in the work lives of middle-aged men* (Vol. 4). Manpower Research Monograph No. 15. Washington, D.C.: U.S. Government Printing Office, 1975.

Parnes, H. S., Nestel, G., Chirikos, T. N., Daymont, T. N., Mott, F. L., Parsons, D. O., & Associates. *From the middle to the later years: Longitudinal studies of the preretirement and postretirement experiences of men* (Vol. 5 in *The Preretirement Years* series). Columbus: Ohio State University, Center for Human Resources, 1979.

Parsons, T. *The social system.* New York: Free Press, 1951.

Pierson, J., & Jaroslovsky, R. Shaky system. *The Wall Street Journal,* June 4, 1979, pp. 1; 24.

Pratt, H. J. Old age associations in national politics. *The Annals of the American Academy of Political and Social Science,* 1974, *415,* 106–119.

Program operations. *Social Security Bulletin,* 1979, *42,* 1–2; 48; 51.

Propping up social security. *Business Week,* July 19, 1976, pp. 34–43.

Quigley, M. W. Executive corps: Free advice pays off for both sides. *Newsday,* June 19, 1979, p. 9.

Quinn, J. F. *The early retirement decision: Evidence from the 1969 retirement history study.* U.S. Department of Health, Education and Welfare, Social Security Administration, Office of Research and Statistics (Staff Paper No. 29). Washington, D.C.: U.S. Government Printing Office, 1978.

Rhine, S. H. *Older workers and retirement.* New York: The Conference Board, 1978.

Rhinelander, P. H. Stereotypes: Their use and misuse. *The Key Reporter,* 1977–1978, *43,* 2–4; 8.

Riegel, K. F., & Riegel, R. M. Development, drop, and death. *Developmental Psychology,* 1972, *6,* 306–319.

Riley, M. W. Aging and cohort succession: Interpretations and misinterpretations. *Public Opinion Quarterly,* 1973, *37,* 35–49.

Riley, M. W. Aging, social change, and the power of ideas. *Daedalus,* 1978, *107,* 39–52.

Riley, M. W., & Foner, A. *Aging and society.* Vol. 1: *An inventory of research findings.* New York: Russell Sage, 1968.

Riley, M. W., Foner, A., Hess, B., & Toby, M. L. Socialization for the middle and later years. In D. A. Goslin (Ed.), *Handbook of socialization theory and research.* Chicago: Rand McNally, 1969.

Riley, M. W., Johnson, M., & Foner, A. *Aging and society.* Vol. 3: *A sociology of age stratification.* New York: Russell Sage, 1972.

Riley, M. W., & Waring, J. Age and aging. In R. K. Merton & R. Nisbet (Eds.), *Contemporary social problems* (4th ed.). New York: Harcourt, Brace, Jovanovich, 1976.

Rosen, B., & Jerdee, T. H. The influence of age stereotypes on managerial decisions. *Journal of Applied Psychology,* 1976, *61,* 428–432.

Rosow, I. *Socialization to old age.* Berkeley: University of California Press, 1974.

Rubin, L. Economic status of black newly entitled workers. In *Reaching retirement age: Findings from a survey of newly entitled workers, 1968–1970.* U.S. Department of Health, Education and Welfare, Social Security Administration, Office of Research and Statistics (Research Report No. 47). Washington, D.C.: U.S. Government Printing Office, 1976.

Schaie, K. W. The primary mental abilities in adulthood: An exploration in the development of psychometric intelligence. In P. B. Baltes & O. G. Brim, Jr. (Eds.), *Life span development and behavior.* New York: Academic Press, 1979.

Schaie, K. W., Labouvie, G. V., & Buech, B. U. Generation and cohort-specific differences in adult cognitive functioning. *Developmental Psychology,* 1973, *9,* 151–166.

Schulz, J. H. The economics of mandatory retirement. *Aging and Work,* 1974, *1,* 1–9.

Schulz, J. H. Income distribution and the aging. In R. H. Binstock, E. Shanas, & Associates (Eds.), *Handbook of aging and the social sciences.* New York: Van Nostrand Reinhold, 1976.

Schwab, D. P., & Heneman, H. G. III. Effects of age and experience on productivity. *Industrial Gerontology,* 1977, *4,* 113–117.

Schwab, K. Early labor-force withdrawal of men: Participants and nonparticipants aged 58–63. In *Almost 65: Baseline data from the Retirement History Study.* U.S. Department of Health, Education and Welfare, Social Security Administration, Office of Research and Statistics (Research Report No. 49). Washington, D.C.: U.S. Government Printing Office, 1976.

Shanas, E. Adjustment to retirement: Substitution or accommodation? In F. M. Carp (Ed.), *Retirement.* New York: Human Sciences Press, 1972.

Shelanski, M. L. The aging brain: Alzheimer's disease and senile dementia. In A. M. Ostfeld & D. C. Gibson (Eds.), *Epidemiology of aging.* U.S. Department of Health, Education and Welfare. Washington, D.C.: U.S. Government Printing Office, 1972.

Sheldon, A., McEwan, P. J. M., & Ryser, C. P. *Retirement: Patterns and predictions.* National Institute of Mental Health, DHEW Publication No. (ADM) 74–49. Washington, D.C.: U.S. Government Printing Office, 1975.

Sheppard, H. L. Work and retirement. In R. H. Binstock, E. Shanas, & Associates (Eds.), *Handbook of aging and the social sciences.* New York: Van Nostrand Reinhold, 1976.

Sheppard, H. L. Factors associated with early withdrawal from the labor force. In S. L. Wolfbein (Ed.), *Men in the pre-retirement years.* Philadelphia: Temple University, School of Business Administration, 1977.

Sheppard, H. L., & Rix, S. E. *The graying of working America: The coming crisis in retirement-age policy.* New York: Free Press, 1977.

Sherman, Sally R. Assets on the threshold of retirement. In *Almost 65: Baseline data from the Retirement History Study.* United States Department of Health, Education and Welfare, Social Security Administration, Office of Research and Statistics. Washington, D.C.: U.S. Government Printing Office, 1976.

Sherman, Sally R. Comparison of aged OASDI and SSI recipients, 1974. *Social Security Bulletin,* 1979, *42,* 40–44.

Sherman, Susan R. Patterns of contacts for residents of age-segregated and age-integrated housing. *Journal of Gerontology,* 1975, *30,* 103–107. (a)

Sherman, Susan R. Mutual assistance and support in retirement housing. *Journal of Gerontology,* 1975, *30,* 479–483. (b)

Shock, N. W., & Norris, A. H. Neuromuscular coordination as a factor in age changes in muscular exercise. In *Medicine and sport.* Vol. 4: *Physical activity and aging.* New York: Karger, Basel, 1970.

Skinner, J. S. Exercise, aging, and longevity. *Proceedings of the 8th Annual Congress of Gerontology* (Vol. 1). Washington, D.C.: Federation of American Societies for Experimental Biology, 1969.

Snee, J., & Ross, M. Social security amendments of 1977: Legislative history and summary of provisions. *Social Security Bulletin,* 1978, *41,* 3–20.

Social security in review. *Social Security Bulletin,* September 1979, *42,* 1; 82.

Streib, G. F., & Schneider, C. J. *Retirement in American society: Impact and process.* Ithaca, N.Y.: Cornell University Press, 1971.

Sumner, W. G. *Folkways.* New York: Dover Publications, 1959.

Thompson, G. B. Work versus leisure roles: An investigation of morale among employed and retired men. *Journal of Gerontology,* 1973, *28,* 339–344.

Thompson, G. B. Pension coverage and benefits, 1972: Findings from the Retirement History Study. *Social Security Bulletin,* 1978, *41,* 3–17. (a)

Thompson, G. B. Impact of inflation on private pensions of retirees, 1970–74: Findings from the Retirement History Study. *Social Security Bulletin,* 1978, *41,* 16–25. (b)

Thompson, W. E. Pre-retirement anticipation and adjustment in retirement. *Journal of Social Issues,* 1958, *14,* 35–45.

Troll, L. E. The family of later life: A decade review. *Journal of Marriage and the Family,* 1971, *33,* 263–290.

Troll, L. E. *Early and middle adulthood.* Monterey, Calif.: Brooks/Cole, 1975.

Uhlenberg, P. Demographic change and problems of the aged. In M. W. Riley (Ed.), *Aging from birth to death.* Boulder, Col.: Westview Press, 1979.

U.S. Bureau of the Census. *Age and race of the population of the United States by state: 1970.* Supplementary Report PC (S1)-13. Washington, D.C.: U.S. Government Printing Office, March 1972. (a)

U.S. Bureau of the Census. *Census of population, 1970: General social and economic characteristics.* Final Report PC (1)-C1; United States Summary. Washington, D.C.: U.S. Government Printing Office, 1972. (b)

U.S. Bureau of the Census. Demographic aspects of aging and the older population in the United States. *Current population reports,* Series P-23, No. 59. Washington, D.C.: U.S. Government Printing Office, May 1976. (2nd printing, revised, January 1978.)

U.S. Bureau of the Census. *Statistical abstract of the United States.* Washington, D.C.: U.S. Government Printing Office, 1977.

U.S. Bureau of the Census. Money income and poverty status of families and persons in the United States: 1978 (Advanced Report). *Current Population Reports,* Series P-60, No. 120. Washington, D.C.: U.S. Government Printing Office, 1979. (a)

U.S. Bureau of the Census. *Statistical abstract of the United States.* Washington, D.C.: U.S. Government Printing Office, 1979. (b)

U.S. Bureau of Labor Statistics. *Comparative job performance by age: Office workers* (Bulletin No. 1273). Washington, D.C.: U.S. Government Printing Office, 1960.

U.S. Department of Commerce. *Social indicators 1976.* Washington, D.C.: U.S. Government Printing Office, 1977.

Walker, J. The job performance of federal mail sorters by age. *Monthly Labor Review,* 1964, *87,* 296–301.

Waring, J. *The middle years: A multidisciplinary view.* New York: Academy for Educational Development, 1978.

Welford, A. T. Motor performance. In J. Birren & K. W. Schaie (Eds.), *Handbook of the psychology of aging.* New York: Van Nostrand Reinhold, 1977.

When retirement doesn't happen. *Business Week,* June 19, 1978, pp. 72–89.

Wikstrom, W. S. *The productive retirement years of former managers.* New York: The Conference Board, 1978.

Wirtz, W. W. The older American worker: Age discrimination in employment, I and II. (Report of the Secretary of Labor). Washington, D.C.: U.S. Government Printing Office, 1965.

Withers, W. Some irrational beliefs about retirement in the United States. *Industrial Gerontology,* 1974, *1,* 23–32.

Yohalem, M. Employee-benefit plans, 1975. *Social Security Bulletin,* 1977, *40,* 19–28.

Name Index

Subject Index

Marital status, 38–39, 103
    and morale, 70–71
Marriage and retirement, 70–72
Morale (*see also* Satisfaction with
        retirement):
    of aged, 105
    and contacts with relatives and friends,
        72–73
    and marital status, 70–71
    of retirees, 104
National Longitudinal Surveys, 48
National Sample Survey, 49
Neighborhood, 40, 41, 73–75
OASDHI, (*see* Social security)
Occupation:
    and job satisfaction, 66
    and retirement, 52
Older workers:
    productivity of, 26–27
    stereotypes of, 28
Organizational membership, 41, 77–78,
        98–99
Organizations of the aged, 77–78, 98–99
Pension (*see also* Social security):
    coverage, 35
    ERISA, 35*n*
    optimum levels of, 94
    trends in receipt of, 76
    vesting of, 35
Planning for retirement, 49–50, 60–62, 71,
        115
Political organization of the aged, 98–100
Population:
    concentration of older persons, 42–43
    fertility, 88–89
    projections, 88–90
Poverty, 34, 94
Productivity of workers, 26–27
Proportion of aged:
    projections about, 89–90
    and reduced isolation of retirees, 79
Public assistance, 34
Race, 36
Reaction time, 25
Relatives, contact with, 40–41, 73
Replacement rates, 33–34
Residential concentration, 42–43
Retirement (*see also* Early retirement;
        Satisfaction with retirement)
    activities in, 39–42, 62–63, 72–73, 77–79
    age, 32–33
    anticipatory socialization for, 60–62
    cohort experience with, 114–115

Retirement (*continued*)
    compulsory, 6, 111–113
    definitions of, 32
    and health, 59
    housing, 73–75
    as life transition, 8, 55–56
    international rates of, 3–4, 5
    and marriage, 70–72
    planning for, 60–61, 71, 115
    as process of social replacement, 110–111
    societal context for, 9–11, 76–79
    trends, 2–7
Role models, 8, 56, 79
Roles:
    continuity of, 40, 42
    discontinuity of, 7–9, 55–57
    marital, 70–72
Satisfaction with retirement, 104–109
    and cohort differences, 108–109
    factors influencing, 57–66, 70–71
    myth of unhappy retiree, 65–66
    sources of variation in, 105–109
Senility, 19–20
Sex comparisons:
    income, 36
    mortality rates, 115
    pension, 35
    satisfaction with retirement, 57*n*
Social networks, 69–73
Social security:
    aggregate benefits paid, 86
    as income source, 34–35, 87
    average benefits, 47–48
    compulsory coverage, 96–97
    future benefit levels, 94–95
    future financing, 9–11, 87–91
    future retirement age, 95
    general revenue financing, 96
    history of, 84–85, 87–88
    political issues, 97–100
    provision of, 85–86
    tax rates, 10, 85–88, 91–94
Stereotypes of older people, 13–18, 28
Strength, muscular, 20–22
Supplementary Security Income, 34
Townsend Movement, 98–99
Volunteer work, 41, 78–79
Widowhood, 38–39, 103
Work:
    and psychological well-being, 56
    among retirees, 36, 42, 58–59, 78–79
Worker-to-retiree ratio, 89